The NATURAL HORSE

Audrey Townley

The Crowood Press

First published in 1993 by
The Crowood Press Ltd,
Ramsbury, Marlborough,
Wiltshire SN8 2HR

British Library Cataloguing in Publication Data

A catalogue record for this book is available from
the British Library.

ISBN 1 85223 742 2

Dedication
To the Brooke Hospital for Animals (Cairo)

Acknowledgements
I am greatly indebted to the following for their contributions to this
book: John Button for his editing; Elsie Paterson for typing the
manuscript; Vivien Dickson for her drawings; Terence Leigh for his
photography; Margot Henley and Catherine Hanbury for allowing
their ponies to be photographed; Deepwater Equitation and Saddlery
Centre; the riders appearing in the photographs; and John Knowles
for his notes on the Przewalski horse.
I should also like to thank all those who allowed me to use their
photographs: John Forbes of Craigievar, The Brooke Hospital for
Animals, The British Horse Society, The Marwell Zoological Park,
and the Glenfarg Group of the Riding for the Disabled Association.

Photographs by Terence Leigh, except where stated in the caption.
Line-drawings by Vivien Dickson.
Diagrams by Annette Findlay.

Typeset by Bookcraft, Stroud, Gloucestershire

Printed in Great Britain by Redwood Books, Trowbridge, Wiltshire

Contents

Preface

The horse has arrived in the present century after a long and remarkable journey that has been, to a great extent, shared with human beings. There is no doubt that the civilization of the human race has been assisted enormously by horse power, and I ask myself what benefits the horse has received in return. It occurs to me that perhaps the wild horse has escaped its role as the victim of natural predators, only to become the victim of human exploitation in one form or another.

The horse has been with us for so long that its presence in our lives is taken for granted, as is its remarkable ability to survive perpetual change in a technological world. In our arrogance, we tend to treat the horse as a lesser form of life, to be bullied or neglected as we see fit. If we can pause from making demands upon the horse for long enough to allow ourselves a period of quiet reflection, we can learn what the horse requires and so improve mutual understanding and respect. Then we can offer it a better quality of life, and in so doing enhance the quality of our own.

The horse is a very special representative of the animal kingdom, but to appreciate that fact fully we need to look at the horse as a whole: at its origins, its instincts and its contribution to the human race past and present. In doing this we can develop a deeper understanding of its physical and psychological needs, and this makes it possible for us to treat it in the holistic way it deserves and not just to concern ourselves with the fragments of its potential that interest us. Only by responding to the horse in this way can we begin to repay some of the outstanding debts that we owe it.

I hope that this book will encourage readers to review their management of the horse, and to look at their relationship with it in a different light. If any of my suggestions provoke thought and prove useful then the book will have served its purpose.

1 The Horse and the Human

When the earth was still young, some 80 million years ago, there was little to suggest that two forms of life would eventually develop and, through their unique relationship, have such a profound effect on the development of the planet. But so it has been with human beings and horses. This millennia-long story of co-operation and interdependence is the theme of this book, the main purpose of which is to remind all who work with horses that the way we relate to our horses today is the result of long centuries of evolution and understanding.

Relating, and the different ways in which we relate, play a very important part in our lives. The poet John Donne reminded us that no one is an island, separate from the rest of existence. This applies no less in our relationships with horses than it does in our relationships with other human beings. Relationships are ongoing experiences, which can be a positive or negative influence in our daily lives. Some degree of insight into the similarities and differences between human and animal relating can help us to utilize these encounters more successfully.

Animals have their own relationship structures, which are specific to particular species and their way of life. Once humans and animals become involved with one another, each with their own faculties for recognition and assessment, some interesting developments can take place.

Social Order

The pecking order, which operates in herd and pack species, provides an organizing system that ensures the species' survival. The young, from their very first days, take their appointed place in this society, and in this way they are first protected and then taught important skills – such as the ability to fend for themselves

The family group.

– by the senior members of the group. This discipline in relating provides security for every animal in the herd.

To a large extent, human children need the same sort of guidance. When a child does not know where it stands, or how far it has to push in order to find the limits of what is acceptable behaviour, it can become very frightened. Temper tantrums are often a plea to parents to establish boundaries which will make the child feel safer. What a child often wants is someone who knows when to say 'No' – and mean it. Sensible, constructive discipline is vital to community harmony, and to an individual's sense of safety. The same principle is operated by the 'boss' horse of the herd or group.

As we grow older, the role of relationships in our lives changes. To begin with the child–parent relationship is the most important, though we may also have important relationships with our brothers and sisters. When we start spending time outside the home, the pupil–teacher relationship becomes important, and later still the relationship between employee and boss. When we ourselves eventually take one of the senior roles – as teacher, employer or parent -- we may well find that the child within us has not completely disappeared. It is well worth trying hard to be aware of which role tends to dominate in our behaviour when confronted with different situations. We can use an understanding of the way these roles work to manipulate situations so that we get what we want.

First Impressions

Relationships are complex, and it is often difficult to analyse why we take to some people and have an antipathy towards others. Why is it that with some horses it is love at first sight, while with others we always have a rather distant relationship?

Empathy.

It is a question of sensing an empathy, a very intuitive form of knowing. I wonder how reliable you find your first impressions of a person – or of a horse. How often have you had to change your perceptions on better acquaintance? It can be fascinating to make a list of your first impressions, then look at them again later and discover how accurate they were.

I tend to back the hunches I get on first acquaintance, but as the years have passed I have discovered that a negative reaction to someone can blind me to that person's positive aspects. We all wear masks, and sometimes these can make us appear unfriendly because of our shyness. This is one advantage that animals have over humans – they do not erect a façade in this way.

I have had a few surprises, and some disappointments, following favourable first impressions. And some of the re-lationships that have followed the less-favourable first impressions have been among my most fulfilling, and these experiences have taught me more about relationships than anything else. The same principle applies to horses: some we like at once, but those who at first seem to be more intractable can sometimes offer us deep and fulfilling relationships; we just need to allow more time to get to know them, and for them to get to know us. Such horses can sometimes turn out to be wonderful performers and friends. A quotation from Richard Bach's *Illusions* sums this up well:

There is
no such thing as a problem
without a gift for you
in its hands.
You seek problems because
you need
their gifts.

Making contact.

The Senses

Animals have acute sensory faculties. Their hearing and sense of smell, for example, are far better than ours. Dogs and horses both use taste when making contact with their own kind or with people, and it is thought that horses also feel vibrations through their feet, which can warn them of approaching friends or foes.

Animals are also much more observant than we realize. Horses and dogs both learn that their owner's change of clothes can indicate when particular activities are about to take place. When horses recognize the pre-hunting routine in the stable and the change of clothes of their riders, they immediately become excited. Still more remarkable is the extraordinary power of perception that is demonstrated by my dogs, who know that they are going to be left at home on a certain day before I have dressed or done anything different from any other day.

There are other senses beyond the five obvious ones, and they are worth considering in the same light. A finely tuned sense of direction enables animals to find their way home over long distances. My own hunters soon orientated themselves to the horsebox when they travelled in it to the meet. They always knew where it was parked at the end of the day, despite being a long way from home in strange surroundings. We human beings do not possess such an accurate radar system, though some of us do have a more highly-developed sense of location and direction than others.

Kinetic sense is the awareness of movement in our muscles, and how this relates to the location of the different parts of our body; it is not quite the same as touch. One way of exploring your kinetic sense is to see how accurately you can bring two fingers slowly together with your arms stretched out and your eyes closed. This important sense is latent in all of us, though the more physical exercise we do the better developed it is likely to be.

Perhaps the sense of temperature is not very different from that of touch, but it is nevertheless an important sense. We use our sense of temperature when feeling for inflammation in a horse's leg when it is lame, or when a child is feverish. Horses cannot tell us when they are feeling the cold any more than a baby can, so knowing when to adjust its clothing to suit the climate depends on your sense of temperature.

When it comes to relating, the senses provide information. Your initial encounter with a stranger may be accompanied by a gut feeling that you like them. Alternatively, you may feel defensive for no obvious reason. Because horses rely more on these senses than most humans do, they are more in touch with information that we find hard to detect. Horses seem to smell fear in humans, and will become upset when a seemingly confident yet deep-seatedly fearful person approaches them. I once had a Great Dane who was extremely docile: only once during his lifetime did he exhibit aggression, and this with one particular man. Why he took exception to this man we never discovered, but the dog refused to let him on the premises.

Body Language

Body language is often crucial when it comes to first impressions. Indeed, although we may not be aware of it, it can be the channel for much of the information we receive from one another. We may be completely unaware of what our posture and gestures tell other people, and they may not be aware that our body language is the source of their reactions. We human beings are not nearly as

Close friends in conversation. (Photo: Angela Stocks.)

9

Positive relationships.

observant as animals, so we do not pick up many of the small nuances that can be so telling. This is particularly relevant when it comes to relating with a horse. We communicate with a horse in the same sort of way as we might with another human being, but we also impose another sort of contact through our bodies, especially when we are mounted. The invisible signals that the horse receives provides very accurate information about the rider's mental and physical attitude.

Body language, unlike the language of words, never lies. Human beings can be taken in by words that mask the 'real' person, and a good actor can interpret a range of personalities very convincingly. The horse, however, always recognizes acting for what it is: our body language always provides it with reliable informa-

tion about the rider's true attitudes and intentions.

The Voice

For humans, one of the most expressive ways of communicating is by using the voice. However, while we can use our voice to give clear information and instructions, it can be misleading if we verbalize our intentions and then contradict them with our body language. This sometimes happens when a person speaks positive words but, at the same time, and often without knowing it, uses body language that is clearly negative. This unconscious shaking of the head or blocking with the hands may indicate that they are not really sure that they believe what they are saying, or want to do what is being suggested. Have you ever wondered how the body language for 'yes' and 'no' evolved as a worldwide code?

Many of the expressions we use to justify our position are contradictory in this way. 'I don't mean to be rude,' for example, usually means you are about to be just that. Your horse will see through these sorts of contradictions: when you give a signal for your horse to canter, for example, but are in fact frightened of cantering. The horse receives the outward signal of your intention, yet it also senses that you are simultaneously countermanding it by tensing parts of your body. You may not realize that you are doing this, but your horse will. This sort of situation is confusing for the horse, and happens more often than riders realize. How the horse copes with this confusion in communication depends very much on the depth of its training, its generosity, and its ability to understand what you really do mean and do it anyway. A sensible horse may be able to work out that although you feel nervous about doing something, you really would like to achieve what you are asking. If this happens you may be blissfully unaware of how co-operative your horse is being.

The voice is a wonderful instrument with which we have been blessed, and in many ways it is an advantage we have over the horse. It enables us to communicate in many complex languages, though perhaps we have developed this ability at the expense of some of our other senses. All of our relationships are enriched by our vocabulary, which constantly extends our frontier of information and understanding in a remarkable way. The range of tone with which we can use our vocal chords can be very expressive of our inner feelings. It is very easy to tell when someone feels tired or depressed from the tone of their voice, and when someone is feeling enthusiastic and exuberant the tone of their voice helps us to share those feelings with them.

An interesting example of the voice's capacity to influence our relationships can arise when a stranger rings us up. Have you noticed your range of reactions to different people in this situation? Do you evoke an imaginary picture of the person to whom you are talking, especially if you find that you feel pleasantly at ease with each other? If you later meet that person face to face, how accurate were your images, and how does that image affect your feelings towards that person when you meet?

Imagining Being the Other

To improve your understanding and appreciation of your relationships, it is often helpful to imagine seeing and hearing yourself in the other person's shoes. This exercise is used in gestalt therapy, a technique which helps people to relate more confidently and to understand other people's points of view. It can help enormously to use a similar exercise when you are with a horse in different situations; putting yourself 'in the horse's shoes' can often help to resolve problem areas in your relationship with the horse.

Your relationship with your horse is very special because of the obvious physical and mental differences between the two species, and a first appraisal tends to highlight these differences. The size of the horse, its superior strength, and its more acute sensory faculties are major differences. The horse's mental and temperamental characteristics would also appear at variance with our own. But at a deeper level there are similarities which we may not always find easy to accept. We might point to the horse's flight, fight or freeze response, behaviour which appears to surface more readily than it does in human beings. If we are honest, however, we may find ourselves admitting that we also react in this way, but we suppress the feelings instead of showing them, often to the detriment of our health.

If we want to relate successfully with the horse, we must first try to understand how it ticks, where it has come from in the evolutionary context, and what it experiences in a contemporary one. If you add these factors to the personality of your horse then you have begun to fill in the background picture of your equine friend, which will almost certainly make you much more tolerant in your attitude to it.

But this is only the first step. I feel we owe it to the horse to review our own behaviour and attitudes, as if we were looking at ourselves from the horse's point of view. We have a tendency to underestimate an animal's ability to assess the situations in which it finds itself, yet, whether we like it or not, their perceptions and reactions are as important as ours. If we learn to recognize what the horse is endeavouring to tell us, the resulting self-analysis and honesty is often both revealing and constructive.

Communication

As we have seen, good relating is very much to do with good communication. As we employ all of our senses to foster the beginnings of a dialogue with the horse,

we may realize that there is a void which needs bridging. Initially this will be done by teaching the horse verbal commands. The human being's initial encounter with the wild horse would have been accompanied by sounds as well as gestures and some sort of basic equipment. It is important for people to speak to their animals regardless of whether they understand or not, because it is the tone of the voice that expresses meaning. Latterly I have become more and more aware that horses respond to quite long sentences of conversation between their owners and me. These sentences do not necessarily contain words of command, yet the animals seem to pick up something of the subjects and intentions being discussed.

I like to think of these lines of communication radiating like a web, which establishes what could be thought of as a 'silent undercurrent of language', and we can reach a point where the conversation between a rider and horse is tactile and mental as well as verbal. When a partnership attains this level of understanding it impinges on the realms of telepathy, when thought alone can initiate a response in both horse and rider.

This experience is, of course, the ultimate in co-operation, and it would be unrealistic to expect all partnerships to work out so harmoniously. It takes all sorts to make a world, and this adage applies to horses as much as it does to humans. It is really only when we have learned to relate with a variety of horses that we become truly adept at meeting each one in the most positive way. The need to be flexible in our relationship with the horse, whose needs can be difficult to understand, puts us to the test in trying to discover the most rewarding ways of working with them.

COMPROMISE

When we understand that the rider's unclear communication is often at the root of conflicts with the horse, it is easier to reduce such conflicts and come to a more useful working arrangement. Not all partnerships are bliss, however, and not all horses are good and co-operative communicators. Once you have worked at establishing clear communications with your horse, it is important to see whether you are prepared to accept the remaining 'problems' in the horse, taking into account both your own priorities and what the horse would choose if it were in your place.

The following story illustrates that horses are no more perfect than humans are, though by learning to communicate well apparent 'faults' can be turned to advantage. David had always wanted to hunt, but the opportunity to do so did not arise until he was running his own business. He then decided to take riding lessons until he was sufficiently proficient to buy his own horse. The one he chose had been a showjumper: it was always keen to be at the front of the field, and was a very bold jumper. The horse's competitive energy made it an impetuous mount to ride, offering a very exciting but rather tiring ride for a novice rider. David, however, persisted with it. He believed that the horse's reliable jumping was a priority, and he could manage to tolerate the more exhausting aspects of his mount.

In the end he had very many happy seasons of enjoyable hunting, and over the years a touching and trusting partnership was achieved. Sadly the time came when at twenty-two years old the horse had to be retired. A younger replacement took the hunter's place, and it was only then that David realized how accustomed he had become to his older horse's impetuous behaviour. When he was asked what he liked best about his new mount, he said it was his calmness.

David had developed a marvellous partnership with his first horse; even though they had a difficult time to begin with, they established a working compromise which gave them both a sense of trust in each other. Now, David is glad to settle for a more tranquil equine personality, and has enough confidence in himself to pass it on to his less experienced horse.

CONNECTING THREADS

All relationships involve communication between the participants: sending and receiving messages in both directions. The more people there are in a group, the more complex is the web of invisible threads that connect them. It is not unlike the network of telephone lines, which criss-cross the country linking everyone together. If we use the setting up of a riding class as an example of the 'spider's web' that these threads weave, we can see what steps can be taken by the coach to ensure that the group lesson has a good chance of nurturing positive relationships. As the picture unfolds, we will see more clearly what can happen when the coach takes the trouble to create a reassuring atmosphere from the start.

The first set of threads is the group's reaction to the coach and, because communication is always in both directions, there is also the coach's reaction to the class as a whole. It is therefore important for the coach to be aware of his or her own appearance, body language, posture, gestures, mannerisms, facial expression and tone of voice.

This might sound like stage management, but it is an important part of the lesson if it is to be constructive. A bright, confident coach with a pleasant opening gambit influences how the group responds, so it is worth the coach taking the trouble to appear this way if a positive response from pupils is desired. The horses, too, are aware of what is happening, even though this is not often realized. Thus the second set of threads is established between the horses and what is going on between coach and pupils. The third set of relationship threads connects the coach with each pupil in the class, and the fourth connects the coach with each of the horses. These can be established quite easily by talking to each pupil about their experiences and problems, and asking about their horses. The fifth thread is between the pupils and their horses, and the conscious acknowledgement of this thread helps riders to be fully aware of their mounts. The sixth thread is that of each of the riders with the others, so introducing everyone to each other will inevitably make the group feel more integrated and comfortable. The seventh and eighth threads are not so obvious, but they exist nevertheless: the seventh is between the horses themselves, and the eighth is between each rider and the horses other than his or her own mount.

If you draw a picture of all these channels of communication, you will see what I mean about the complexity of the web of relationships within a group. They multiply very quickly to add up to a surprising total. No wonder the quality of these relationships has such a significant effect on the mood of the class.

It needs only one spanner in the works to spoil the comfortable flow of accord which can make working together so

mutually supportive and productive. This process of getting to know each other may take just a little more time before teaching can get under way, but it will be made up once the class has been prepared and work begins. This period at the beginning of each session might be looked upon as 'the positive introduction', and can be consolidated by giving a brief outline of the proposed lessons so that the class is reassured by knowing what is likely to take place.

These preparations need not be confined to riding; they can be useful whenever people are in contact with one another – in the workplace, at school, within the family, or in team sports. In riding circles, however, the presence of the horse provides an extra dimension to our experience of relating. In your horse you have a fair-minded referee, and a very accurate assessor. This can be a very illuminating experience, and one through which you can gain more insight into the different facets of your personality. When you discover them and use these insights constructively, you will become a more balanced and well-rounded person.

BUILDING A VOCABULARY

For a relationship to be successful, the development of a common language must inevitably take place. Our human ability to speak to one another is not always a reliable means of exchanging information, for we love to exaggerate and embellish, and we often hear only what we want to hear. Then we find it hard to admit that we have not understood, and muddle on pretending that we have.

If these problems can arise with human beings who speak a common language, they are increased when different nationalities try to converse. Perhaps you can recall an occasion when you felt like an alien in a strange country. This happened to me once in Vienna, when a friend and I left the group we were with to do some shopping, and lost our way. We could find no one who spoke English, and it was only with considerable difficulty that we managed to retrace our steps. In retrospect we found this experience amusing, but at the time the feeling was closer to panic. It can pose problems when we try to speak to people of another nationality; if we remember this, we will appreciate better what it must be like for a horse.

The young horse's education in communication starts when its carefree days of youth come to an end. Just how this proceeds depends on the circumstances in which it finds itself. If it is in the hands of a dealer who wants a quick turnover, the education may be cursory or demanding. On the other hand, the young horse that finds itself with a skilful trainer will have a better chance of acquiring an understanding of the basics of communication.

The horse that graduates in this way will learn the words of command and the signals that will in time make up a considerable vocabulary of human/equine language. As a result, its performance and temperamental stability will have every chance of improvement. Sadly, many horses do not receive such a sound education, and end up feeling confused, frightened, or simply bored. This can easily lead to conflict with their riders, who do not appreciate the dilemma in which the horse finds itself. As the owner of one riding school recently said to me, it is hard to purchase a really well-educated and well-mannered horse, and I had to agree.

For a horse that has not learned the basics of education when it is young, reschooling, and the building up of a language which the horse understands, is vital. It is only in this way that its physical condition can be improved. This process cannot be hurried: proper training exercises must be followed for months and even years before the learning is consolidated in the horse's mind and body.

Expectations

When training problems do arise, it is easy to make false assumptions about the reasons for them. It is tempting to get angry when the horse appears disobedient, when in fact it is frightened, confused or just tired. Another reason for the conflict can be the rider's unrealistic goals, and riders often get in the horse's way by losing their patience. Before you blame the horse, it is always worth checking your motives to make sure that it is not you who are out of balance, or giving the wrong message.

When you become involved with a new horse, as with a new person, it helps if you have some background information which puts you in the picture and makes for easy and appropriate conversation. You may as a result discover reasons for that horse's behaviour towards you, which can help you to be more tolerant when the horse appears indifferent or inhibited. Here are three case histories showing how early experiences in a horse's life can affect their later ability to learn communication skills.

Donna, a bay mare, was bought by a riding school because the owners were saddened by her condition when they saw her at a sale. Her conformation was not her strong point: in her debilitated state

15

she looked more like a kipper than a horse. Her large honest eyes and friendly disposition, however, were so appealing that they decided to buy her. When Donna was strong enough to work, she was found to be unschooled and, though she was anxious to please, she was very tense. With patience, not only did she return to full health, but she blossomed into a very handsome cob that was held in great affection by all who knew her, even during the difficult days of her education. Once Donna's confidence was consolidated and she understood what she was being taught, she began to enjoy her work and was much in demand, thus repaying her owners many times over.

The second example is an event mare that I purchased as a five-year-old for fifty pounds, because she had become unmanageable in the hunting field. I owe this horse's improvement to the late Captain Edy Goldman, whose particular forte was horses with this type of temperament. What I learnt from him about my mare and myself has stood me in good stead ever since. Apart from her son, she became the best horse I ever owned. Her versatility in the show ring, as a working hunter, and as an eventer gave me much pleasure over the years.

The time came when I decided to breed from her, and chose to send her to a well-known stallion some distance away. When I went over to collect the horse, six weeks later, I was appalled to find the mare, a shadow of her former self, standing dejectedly in a tumbledown barn. I suspected that there was also a shortage of water, which would help to account for her poor condition. Luckily, she was not in foal, and within two months we managed to improve her physical condition; her mental state, however, gave cause for concern. It was as if her spirit had been broken, and she had sunk into an acute depression. This was so different from her normal *joie de vivre* that it was difficult to believe that she was the same horse that I had sent away. It took more than six months for her to climb back to anything like her former self, and even longer to regain her usual liveliness. I found it very difficult to forgive myself for what had happened to her while out of my hands.

The third story is about a high-class show hack, which I acquired because it had become what is known as 'ring-sour'. Any horse can choose to switch off and resent its work if it becomes too repetitive and stressful; but this beautiful horse was not only sick of the show ring, it had also turned away from human contact. When out riding he was always well behaved if excitable, but his lack of interest in human contact was very evident.

Eventually I decided to send him to my second stable yard, run by a very competent young member of my staff, where the hunters were kept. She eventually managed to establish a rapport, which began to change this horse in a remarkable way. The true personality of this charming horse began to emerge, and the result was quite amazing. His dull indifferent body language became more alert as his trust in people grew and he found relationships with them rewarding. This horse spent the rest of his life in my possession, returning to the show ring occasionally with good grace, and he became one of the most popular horses with my pupils.

Horse Talk

Teaching the horse to understand and obey directions is how we begin to communicate with it in order to gain control. This should be done patiently, and with simplicity and logical progression. There are a few very special trainers who have an uncanny ability to handle an unbroken horse within a matter of hours, but these individuals are rare communicators. Usually the procedure takes much longer, and any short cuts spoil the chances of discovering the horse's real potential. The art is to develop the pupil's natural aptitude, which will only take place if:

a horse is interested;
it understands;
there is feedback;
there is a good relationship with the
    teacher;
the horse is in good health.

This last factor is very important and often ignored. Perhaps this is because we often accept for ourselves a second-rate sense of well-being rather than optimum vitality.

When a horse is being trained, the role of the teacher is vital and usually dominant. Let us not forget, however, that we can also learn important lessons from the horse as its education proceeds. We do need to direct it and be in charge of operations, but not to the exclusion of our own awareness of what the horse is trying to tell us. We need to listen and learn from the horse's body language – what I call 'horse talk'. I am sure they must find humans the most irritating and incessant chatterboxes! A little more observation and a little less talking on our part would give the horse more breathing space. Sometimes you can almost hear them saying, 'For goodness sake, shut up for a moment and give me a chance to think.'

How do we talk to the horse so that the conversation flows and our work together shows some progress? The horse knows when it gets something right, because it senses your pleasure. It thus receives a reward for its efforts, and this should make it feel more comfortable doing its work. The key to this way of working lies in following a straightforward sequence, which goes as follows:

1. Give a clear signal which the horse understands. For example, if you are teaching it to walk on to a voice command, you can encourage it to move forward by walking forward with it.
2. As it succeeds in doing what is asked, cease giving the signal.
3. Implement the reward: a word of flattery, a pat, or even a rest.

You can then repeat the process, until little by little the horse walks on freely. I call this the request–response–reward sequence, or the 'three Rs'. In time your ever more complex signals, fully understood by the horse, enable it to perform difficult manoeuvres with spontaneous ease. Remember that this sequence is the basis of your conversation with the horse at all levels of training. A useful little phrase to remember is, 'When I ask, I also give.' What you are giving is encouragement and thanks. You ask for something until you receive a response from the horse, and then you thank the horse for doing it. This keeps you aware and in tune, so that you never take what the horse is giving for granted or expect it to continue giving for too long. We do have a tendency to be greedy about keeping good results going.

When we implement this procedure, we begin to understand how the horse talks to us, and how the lines of com-

17

munication develop as they become more established. The horse is not a verbal creature in the same sense that we are, and it has to express its moods and its difficulties with its body language. Someone once said to me that the horse has such an expressionless face. I do not think that they had spent much time watching one. Although the horse's face may appear immobile, this is a false impression as anyone who has studied them will know.

The horse's sensitive ears are constantly flicking back and forth, and this is the first thing to which you should pay attention. The ears are constantly telling a story as they move; the range of messages is varied and changes rapidly. I think of the horse's ears as providers of subtle information, and you can play a fascinating game by verbally translating the nuances of your horse's ear movement. See whether you understand what the various angulations mean, and see if you can keep up with the information that they are relaying from moment to moment.

One horse I was schooling had a habit of laying its ears back to demonstrate its intense irritability whenever I used my legs. My aim was to respond with a relaxed attitude in order to avoid compounding the conflict. When the horse refused to go forward I waited for it to relax before giving another signal. I was ready to reward its smallest attempt to make a step. With this encouragement the horse began to move forward in a happier frame of mind. When it did begin to move I made sure that I gave it a reward before repeating the signal. Eventually I had some success with this approach; the horse started to move forward, flicking its ears in a much more alert way. When this happened, its body began to relax. An onlooker thought the horse had become

The pony on the left is showing an interest in the mare.

The mare's ears and tail show disapproval.

The mare decides to make friends. Notice the rider's body language.

inattentive, and was listening to extraneous activities, but this was not so. In this horse's case, when its ears were pricked forward it moved much more comfortably and confidently. A horse which flattens its ears against its poll is very tense at that moment, as an overall view of the rest of its body will demonstrate.

The eyes of the horse can tell us a story too. They can be bright, alert, big, liquid and very appealing. On the other hand they can be wild and frightened, small and piggy. They can convey health, fatigue and illness. When a horse is off-colour, the eyes seem to sink into the socket and the hollow above the eye seems more pronounced; the overall effect is of the eye becoming small and rather dull.

You may not think there is much left on the horse's face to tell us about its state of being, but we must not omit the muzzle and nostrils, which are so flexible. Touch and smell are the important senses located in this area of the horse's anatomy. Horses use their lips and tongue to investigate other horses, people and objects. The whiskers are very sensitive, and the horse gets important information from them, especially in the dark; they really should not be deprived of this information by having them trimmed.

The rest of its body, too, plays its part. The horse paws with the forefeet, kicks with the hind, and its tail is a wonderful barometer of tension and relaxation. When a horse is tense it will swish its tail back and forth; when relaxed it will let it swing softly with its gaits. In this way, the tail provides the dressage judge with valuable information during a competition. We can learn to read our horse's body like a book.

When your horse does give vent vocally, it is usually because its friends are

Making friends during a photography session.

Investigating.

absent, or it is pleased to see you appear at feeding time. Some horses have an endearing habit of giving a soft whinny when they see their owners, which has nothing to do with food. This is a particularly pleasing gesture, which can make you feel the recipient of a specially intimate compliment from the horse. It is literally talking to you in its own language. When this happens you are experiencing the relationship with your horse at the highest level.

2 Genesis

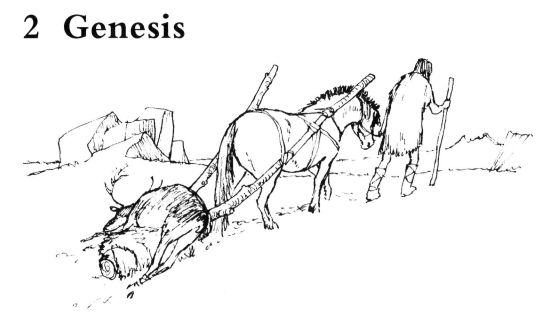

When God created the horse, He said 'I have made Thee unlike any other. All the treasures of the earth lie between Thine eyes. Thou shalt cast mine enemies between Thy hooves, but Thou shalt carry my friends on Thy back. This shall be the seat from which prayers rise unto me. Thou shalt find happiness all over the earth and Thou shalt be favoured above all other creatures, for to Thee shall accrue the love of the Master of the Earth. Thou shalt fly without wings and conquer without sword.'

From an English translation of *The Koran*, London 1880

The horse is one of nature's oldest and most successful products. For anyone who has the welfare of the horse at heart it can help enormously to have some understanding of the horse's ancient lineage, for I believe that such knowledge can deepen our appreciation of this remarkable species. Its history has been recounted many times, but it always bears retelling, since it has a significant bearing on our contact with the horse in the present.

Horses, like humans, still possess some very ancient needs and instincts, and it can help us enormously if we can recognize them. When there is misunderstanding between horse and human, it is always worth asking ourselves whether it might be echoes of our relationship in the distant past that we are reawakening.

I shall not dwell on the minor links in the chain of equine history lest this leads to confusion, but shall include only the vital stages of the horse's development.

The Origins of the Horse

Life in its simplest form existed more than 3,000 million years ago, but the period we are most interested in is the Mesozoic era, about 136 million years ago, when the giant reptiles were lords of all they surveyed. At that same time, however, there were also early prototype mammals, including some small insect-eating creatures which lived in trees. One of the little herbivorous mammals that darted about in the undergrowth has been given the name *Pantothere*. *Pantothere* is considered by many palaeontologists to be the progenitor of the horse, although it would diversify many times before its particular speciality would be consolidated. Remains of this humble creature have been found in North America, among other places.

It is thought that another small tree creature from this period was the ancestor of the apes and, as such, could have been the forerunner of humankind. These two species, living together in the trees of the Mesozoic era so many million years ago, may seem unlikely antecedents of humans and horses, but their existence indicates that we have been living alongside each other for a great deal longer than you may imagine.

The dinosaurs held sway for 35 million years, making them one of nature's most successful creations. There are various theories about their mysterious and sudden demise, though it is now believed that some widespread catastrophe overtook the planet, wiping out most living things. It is certainly the case that when fossil dinosaur skeletons have been excavated, they have often been covered with a layer of earth holding no evidence of life at all. In levels above this barren stratum, however, fossils of elephants, camels and even horses are often found, suggesting that it did not take nature long to find a replacement for the dinosaurs.

Another little-known predecessor of the horse, a 'missing link' in its prehistory, is also thought to have existed. Researchers have built up a picture of what it looked like, even though there is no fossil evidence to prove it. This as yet unproven animal is sometimes referred to as *Palaeohippus*, but until there is some proof of its existence it has no official name. Its legs are thought to have shown the beginnings of elongation, which would eventually become the distinguishing feature of the early horse.

THE DAWN HORSE

The next stage of our drama is a significant one in the horse's evolution. It begins during the Eocene period, about 55 million years ago, with *Eohippus*, also known as *Hyracotherium* or 'the dawn horse' (*eos* is the Greek word for 'dawn'). Unlike *Palaeohippus*, fossil evidence of *Eohippus* is plentiful, both in North America where it is thought to have originated, and in Europe, where it may have migrated across the land bridge which connected the two continents at that time.

Eohippus was not much larger than a cat, and lived in the undergrowth where it browsed on leaves. The most significant aspects of the evolution of the horse are found in its dentition and in its feet. At this stage *Eohippus* had four hoofed toes

An artist's impression of Eohippus.

23

and a pad on its front legs, and three hoofed toes and a pad on its hind ones. The arrangement of *Eohippus*'s forty-four teeth was characteristic, and gives us a clue to its future destiny. Though there were changes in the quality of the teeth, the construction of the horse's mouth has been a constant factor throughout its evolution, their number and placing remaining the same in the species which were to follow. Gradually *Eohippus* became larger in size, and its legs grew longer as it adapted to a changing environment.

The next major change came with the arrival of *Mesohippus* about 35 million years ago. This creature had more durable teeth than *Eohippus*, but more important is the change that had taken place in its feet. This animal had three hoofed toes and a weight-bearing central pad, and its legs had already become longer so that it stood about 6hh or 24in (61cm) at the withers. The 1990 Year of the Horse exhibition in Glasgow included a model of *Mesohippus*, which had a recognizable horse-like appearance and was bay in colour with a donkey-like tail. It reminded me very much of the lovable character Eeyore in A.A. Milne's *Winnie the Pooh*.

The successor to *Mesohippus*, appearing some 25 million years ago, was *Merychippus*. The emergence of this savannah horse, adapted to the grasslands that were opening up as the forests receded, represented a dramatic leap forward. This animal had better teeth which grew from the roots, and which could cope with grazing and chewing grass. The two side toes were reduced so that the central part of the foot took the animal's weight on its hoof-like structure. *Merychippus* stood 10hh or 40in (102cm) high, and was to be very important in equine lineage.

The grazing horses of the prairies continued to evolve successfully, and some of them migrated overland to Africa and South America. About 25 million years ago *Hipparion*, the last of the three-toed horses, is thought to have died out. There is some suggestion that it may have had a striped coat.

The next major step in the horse's evolution came with the arrival of *Pliohippus* about ten million years ago. *Pliohippus* had four single hooves and no visible side toes (vestiges of the prehistoric toes can be seen as the splint bones on the leg of the modern horse and in the chestnut which lies at the back of the fetlock joints). *Pliohippus* was beginning to resemble the horse as we know it today.

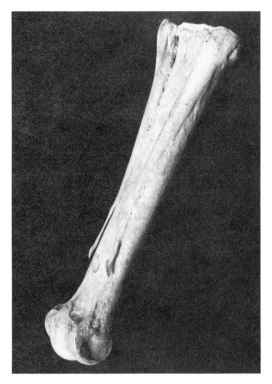

Splint bones on either side of the cannon bone.

Then, about one million years ago, another extremely important character in our drama appeared: *Equus*, the direct antecedent of our present-day horse.

EQUUS

Equus, like its immediate predecessor, had hoofs instead of toes. But *Equus* was bigger and probably reached 12hh or 48in (122cm), or even 14hh or 56in (142cm). The genus *Equus* is made up of a number of species, including *Equus caballus*, generally believed to be the direct antecedant of the domestic horse.

It had taken the horse 60 million years to evolve from *Eohippus*, just 9in high at the withers, to *Equus caballus*, now standing more than 4ft tall. Put side by side, these two animals would bear very little resemblance to one another. Like *Eohippus*, *Equus* is thought to have originated in North America, migrating to South America, and eventually reaching Africa, Asia and Europe over the land bridge which still joined these continents. *Equus* in North America became extinct about 10,000 years ago, although the reasons for this remain a mystery. It is through the herds that migrated to other continents that *Equus* was able to survive, and it was not until 1519 that horses were reintroduced to America by the Spaniards. These horses became the foundation stock of the feral herds that still exist in that country.

As *Equus* adapted to changes of climate, terrain and grazing it became more diversified. Evidence of these primitive ancestors can still be seen in the zebra markings on the legs of Highland and Norwegian ponies and in the dorsal stripe down their backs. The complexity of diversification that the *Equus* genus has undergone is demonstated by the representatives that still survive today: the przewalski; the African wild ass; the Asiatic wild ass; and the zebra.

The przewalski, *Equus przewalskii* Poliakoff, also called the Asiatic or Mongolian wild horse, is named after the colonel who first introduced it to the western world in 1880. Even then only a few small herds existed, and the species was saved from extinction only by capturing some of them for breeding in captivity. A significant difference between the przewalski and other horses is that it has two additional chromosomes, making it a distinct species rather than just a subspecies. While the przewalski is a distinct species, it will crossbreed with domestic species. In the past, in Mongolia, the przewalski may have been crossbred to create an animal with enormous stamina for racing.

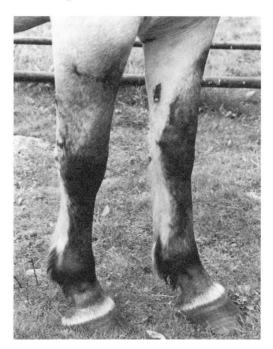

Zebra markings.

25

Dorsal stripe on a crossbred Norwegian pony.

The wild tarpan, which is now extinct, lived in the steppes and forests of southern Russia and eastern Europe; until the eighteenth century it was widely hunted. Although it was extremely hardy, impervious to colds and coughs, and reputed never to abort, it was supposedly untameable, though I have read that it was used as a draught horse in some areas. Unfortunately it was extinct by the twentieth century, though the Polish konik ('little horse') may be a descendant. There have been several unsuccessful attempts to recreate the tarpan in eastern Europe.

Both the przewalski and the tarpan are distinguished by their short chunky legs and rather large heads. The mountain breeds tend to have shorter legs than their counterparts living on flatter terrain; the latter depend more on their long legs, designed for speed, for their survival.

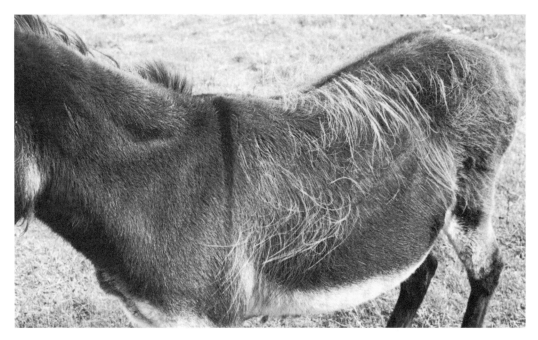

Dorsal and vertical stripes form a cross on a donkey.

26

There are two species of African wild ass. The Nubian is now thought to be extinct, though there are crosses with domestic asses to be seen today which still bear the characteristics of the wild ass. The other species is the Somali wild ass, to be found in arid areas in Somalia and parts of Ethiopia; it is now a protected species, with an uncertain future in that troubled part of the world. It is likely that the contemporary domestic donkey is descended from the Nubian wild ass.

The story of the Asiatic wild ass is more complex. Two types, also known as onagers, are usually recognized: the Persian onager and the Turkmenian onager. There is still a healthy population of the latter in Turkmenistan. Travelling eastwards towards Mongolia we find similar breeds, the dziggetai and the kiang, both of which have rather large heads. Further south, in India and Pakistan, is the khur, a smaller form of wild ass than the other

Przewalski. (Photo: Marwell Zoological Park.)

A thirty-year-old Norwegian mare whose forebears go back to the Ice Age.

27

onagers, and another possible ancestor of the modern domestic donkey.

The zebra is technically of the *Equus* genus, but there has been no demand for its domestication.

THE MODERN HORSE

It is possible that the primitive horses that were derived from *Equus*, and were eventually to become domesticated, interbred when opportunity or necessity prevailed. This would continue with human intervention and the results would eventually be recognizable in horses like the Suffolk Punch, the Arab and the Clydesdale. Selective breeding probably reached its zenith and commercial value with the development of the Thoroughbred. This breed owes much to the introduction of Arabian sires, such as the Byerley Turk, the Godolphin and the Darley Arabian.

Any discussion of the origins of the modern horse must include more than a passing mention of the Arab, an animal which has had such a profound effect on so many breeds, especially Britain's Thoroughbred stock. Legends and facts often become confused, and this certainly seems to be true when it comes to the origins of the Arab horse. Bedouins believe it existed 30,000 years ago; Lady Wentworth thought it was a separate species. There is no doubt, however, that the

Suffolk Punches at work.

The Thoroughbred.

Arab's characteristics are distinct and very dominant. Perhaps this horse's particular qualities were enhanced by its close association with Arab families, whose respect and care for the horse was equalled only by the Native Americans.

British native ponies are said to have migrated from Europe when the British Isles was part of the Continent. The

The Arab.

Exmoor pony is said to resemble the Gotland Russ, and the Fell pony the Friesian horse. The Shetland has been depicted in cave paintings, and its small size would have made it a relatively easy animal to transport. It was probably the Beaker people, who also brought with them the arts of pottery and metalwork, who brought the Shetland to Britain.

Domestication

There is no clear evidence to suggest when the horse was first domesticated, and estimates vary enormously. Some historians suggest that the Persians were horsemen in the third millennium BC, while others place the horse's domestication much more recently. *The Guinness Book of Records*, for example, places it in the Ukraine some 6,500 years ago, though it

An ivory Persian pendant.

29

then appears to contradict itself by suggesting that there is evidence of crib-biting by tethered horses in the south of France from 30,000 years ago. (I find it interesting that this symptom of stress, still found in the modern horse, should have appeared so early in its shared history with human beings.)

As with so many things, I think it depends upon what we mean by 'domestication'. If it means any use of the horse for human purposes then it is possible that it was during the early Stone Age, between 50,000 and 100,000 years ago, that the horse first became domesticated. The horse or pony depicted in cave paintings is often shown as a victim of the chase, falling to an arrow or spear, and at some point humans realized they could catch and keep horses in order to provide food as and when they needed it.

As the ice receded after the last Ice Age, vegetation started to re-establish itself and early forms of settled agriculture spread across Europe and Asia. At some point the horse assumed a different role, and became, either by accident or inspiration, a haulier. Harnessing horse power must have been one of the first and most significant labour-saving discoveries. Primitive sledges in the form of a 'V', similar to those used by Indians, may have been used. The first draught horses, some 3,000 years ago, were onagers. Early Egyptian and Greek sources show the horse pulling chariots some time before there is any evidence of the horse being ridden. The Egyptians have left us pictorial evidence of ornately harnessed horses for pulling elaborate chariots. The Hittites, in around 2000BC, left records on stone tablets of horse management and instruction. The Chinese were also riding horses in the second millennium, and rock drawings depict mounted archers, perhaps riding descendants of the przewalksi wild horse.

The Romans were slow to convert their

The King's Troop of the Royal Horse Artillery.

marching legions into cavalry, but eventually they were forced to change their tactics to avoid being outwitted by mounted enemies who rode without stirrups. For many centuries it was the versatility and speed of the ridden horse which brought the use of cavalry to the fore on the battlefield. It is a sad fact that right up to the First World War millions of horses were sent into the war zone to become victims of human destructiveness.

It is appropriate here to consider how the native tribes of North America acquired and learnt to ride the feral horses that were reintroduced to the New World by the Spanish in 1519. North American Indians did not acquire horses for themselves until the early 1700s but, once they had done so, they became superb riders, using only the minimum of equipment. They controlled their horses with a loop of rope or rawhide round the lower jaw of the horse and a single rein. They rode bareback, and could direct the horse without this rein, so that both their hands could be kept free.

The North American Indian.

Travelling Companions

Considering how much we owe to the horse, it seems sad that we have often treated it with the same disregard with which we have treated many of the world's other animal species.

At one time, the horse was hunted for food, which seems ironic when you consider that nowadays the horse often carries the hunter. The rarity of breeds such as the przewalski, and the extinction of the tarpan, are largely a result of relentless hunting. There are records from France that suggest that ancient tribes killed large herds of horses by stampeding them over cliff edges. The wastage and suffering of injured animals must have been appalling. Another hunting method was to panic herds into dead-end gullies where they made easy prey for the hunters because they trampled each other to death. How, you may ask, can we ever repay our debt to the horse, and how can reconciliation be possible after the horse has experienced such persecution?

Perhaps this journey into the past will put the horse into true perspective, helping to explain some of its instinctive behaviour and special needs. The horse has a unique place in the saga of evolution. It is one of the few animals to boast such a long history and, until the invention of forms of transport based on fossil fuels, it was the primary means of transport for people and goods alike – a role it still plays in many poorer countries.

This wonderful creature has outlived many other forms of life and, like the ugly duckling, has come out of the past with the grace of a swan for all of us to enjoy.

3 Educating the Horse

From the earliest days of the horse's domestication, 'submission' has been the word most often used in its training. With the exception of a few enlightened masters, history records the use of force in equine training throughout the ages. Xenophon the Greek was one of the first to write a treatise on using gentleness with horses, and the following quotation illustrates his beliefs:

The hand must be neither held so strict as to confirm and make the horse uneasy, nor so loosely as not to let him feel it. The moment he obliges and answers it, yield the bridle to him. This will take off the stress and relieve his bars [bits] and conforms to the maxim which should not be forgotten, which is to caress him and reward him for whatever he does well. The moment that the rider perceives that the horse begins to place his head, to go lightly in the hand and with ease and pleasure to himself [the rider] I should do

nothing that is disagreeable but flatter and coax him to rest a while and do all he can to keep the horse in his happy temper. This will encourage and prepare him for greater understanding.

The history of the horse's education was influenced by historical events. In Greece, the art of horsemanship had reached the level of high school by at least 400BC. The frieze on the Parthenon of the Acropolis in Athens depicts high school movements, movements that are very difficult for the horse to execute to order with the weight of a rider on its back, though they are seen in horses at liberty when they rear, leap or prance about in high-stepping trot. 'High school' means that the horse can produce these difficult movements in perfect balance when it is being ridden. It takes years rather than months to train a horse to this level, and horses of this calibre were often used in battle because of their agility.

A nation's cultural level seems to influence its standard of horsemanship. With the downfall of the Greek civilization, the standard of riding went into its own dark age. The Romans were unenthusiastic horsemen, preferring other ways of utilizing the horse, chariot racing being one example. The Middle Ages brought the demand for big, robust horses to carry knights in armour, for jousting or battle. It was the advent of small firearms that again changed the type of horses required for military purposes; it now needed to be agile, small and obedient. At the turn of the fifteenth century the Italians seem to have taken the lead in this respect. Frederico Grisone established the first riding academy in Naples. This drew pupils from far and wide, so he opened another school in Rome. He also wrote a book called *Ordine Cavalcare*, published in 1550. From there the art of high school riding spread to France through Salomon

Playing.

de la Broue and, perhaps more importantly, Anton de Pluvinel de Baume. Both had been trained in Italy by one of Grisone's pupils.

Through these pioneers, France now became more dominant in the art of train-

Knight in armour.

33

*The capriole. The Spanish Riding School.
Note, no throat lash, no stirrups!*

ing horses and riders. Pluvinel seems to have made a particular name for himself as a trainer. He was against all forms of brutality, and saw the horse as a thinking creature who needs encouragement and reward. He forged a special relationship with the young Louis XIII, and wrote a book on riding for him.

Great Britain seems to have been more reluctant to make equestrian changes, perhaps because the sporting aspect of riding was more important. The Duke of Newcastle (1592–1676), who was an enthusiastic high school exponent, met with little success in trying to convert his countrymen. His methods were thought to be harsh, artificial and reactionary.

In 1796, François Rubichon, Sieur de la Guérnière, opened a riding academy in Versailles, where he became renowned for his training methods, which were sound and humane. He had an empathy with his

horses, and he evolved new exercises which helped to improve the standard of training. François Baucher (1796–1873) had his followers, and James Fillis, an Englishman (1834–1913) also made an important contribution to training methods. Both these trainers were involved with the training of circus horses. Fillis also influenced military riding, and taught horses artificial movements that had no place in classical riding.

La Guérnière's chief success lay in the influence he had on the training fundamentals of the Spanish Riding School. This school dates back to the sixteenth century, and has become the home of classical riding in its purest form. People of all ages, nations and walks of life queue daily to catch a glimpse of this superb spectacle of horsemanship. The beautiful baroque hall in which the gala performances take place was completed in 1735.

'Breaking In' or 'Training'?

History has shown that brute force is not the answer to a horse's education, though its use is still all too frequent. Maybe, being in some ways a rather puny rival to the horse, we humans sometimes feel we need to augment this physical discrepancy. The result has been the invention of some devilish devices, capable of inflicting great pain on the horse. Another technique of domination is to exhaust the horse in order to subdue it. This can involve exercise, or depriving the horse of food and water. No wonder the term 'breaking in' has become the standard; a new and more humane term for the humane methods now employed has yet to be coined.

The word 'training' is confusing partly because of its use in the racing world, where it has long been used to describe fitness regimes. I use the word 'education', because this is, after all, the object of the exercise.

Teacher and Pupil

Education is not possible without communication, concentration and understanding. The educator needs to have an empathy with the horse, a complete understanding of the schooling procedure, and great patience and calmness. The process involves tactics more akin to the martial arts, using the principles of non-resistance.

This does not mean that we should let the pupil run rings round us, for at times a certain firmness or persistence is necessary to make progress. Unfortunately the concept of 'discipline' in this day and age has become very negative, and partly as a reaction against limiting ideas about discipline we see an increase in unruly behaviour all round us. What discipline provides us with, when we use the idea correctly, is a framework which produces an underlying sense of security and direction. The horse, or the child for that matter, knows where they stand.

A conversation I recently had with a school teacher will help to illustrate my point. I asked her what she thought about discipline. She said it was absolutely essential, but she thought of it as benign rather than active. She explained how she could control assembly at school by simply walking on to the platform and asking the pupils to be quiet, while other teachers resorted to shouting at them, usually to no avail. I asked her what she thought was the difference between the two methods. This question momentarily nonplussed her, as she had taken her authority for granted. I suggested that maybe her body language emanated confidence, and after thinking about it for a second or two she agreed. The horse trainer, too, can often achieve better results by using psychological tactics rather than physical ones.

When we assume the role of teacher we must, like any good schoolteacher, know our subject. I frequently have riders coming to me with their problem horses, only to find that they have not begun to teach their horse basic manners. Just like children, horses must be taught the equivalent of the 'three Rs' before more advanced education begins. If this omission is not rectified before lungeing the horse, it will inevitably lead to evasions and resistance, making lungeing lessons difficult. Of all the horses with which I begin work, only a minority will have been taught the language of voice and subtle whip signals to the point of reliable obedience. The majority of horses lunge their trainers. Riding a horse with such a fragile foundation to its education, expecting it to behave well and to mature, is unrealistic and unfair to the horse.

It is important to remember that the primary instinct of the natural horse is its instinct for survival, which is still innate even in domesticated horses.

This insight can help the trainer to anticipate problems and, when they do arise, deal with them in an appropriate and logical way, which the horse can understand. The effective trainer needs to plan a programme that is within the horse's range of mental and physical ability, and have the necessary equipment to be able to lunge the horse correctly and safely.

Time to Talk

An appreciation of the vocabulary that the horse has to learn before communication is established is vital. When they are taught by an experienced handler, who also has endless patience, calmness and tact, many horses can increase their vocabulary to an extremely complex level. Time is on your side if you learn to value and trust this important principle. The important thing to remember is 'There is always tomorrow'. Too many misunderstandings spring from expecting the horse to learn too much at once and for too long, and the same applies to ourselves. Ten minutes is often quite long enough for early lessons.

I always remember my first encounter with the Chinese martial art of *t'ai chi*, when the instructor did not consolidate the previous lesson before embarking on the next. I was utterly bewildered, and felt an intense desire to shout out, 'For goodness sake, give us time and stop overloading us.' This experience taught me how horses must often feel, and how careful I must be to give my riders and horses enough time to build up confidence in each stage of the lesson. It is no good moving forward too quickly if you are unsure of the first steps. We all tend to succumb to the pressure of time, not realizing that short cuts simply will not work: we become victims of time, taking the horse with us, instead of using time to our mutual benefit. When we do take time to consolidate the learning, it is surprising how much more observant and intuitive we become. An unhurried atmosphere sets up an entirely different energy, to which the sensitive horse readily responds, because it recognizes the absence of anxiety in its trainer.

Conditions for Learning

If the horse is to accept its training with the minimum of trauma and stress, certain preconditions must be fulfilled. Before serious lessons commence, the horse should be prepared, both in the stable and when being led. If it is fortunate enough to be in good hands, this nursery education can start quite early in its life.

To teach the horse to obey the words 'Walk', 'Trot' and 'Halt' does not take long, and should be done from both sides when standing or leading it. In the stable the horse will learn to accept handling, grooming and the requests 'Move over' or 'Stand back' when box doors are opened. A light reprimand with the voice should be used if the young horse becomes cheeky or bossy, maybe even a very light tap with the hand to show your disapproval, but this should never be at the expense of lost confidence.

Many people do not realize how long it takes for a horse to reach full maturity. Its bones do not become fully formed until it is about five years old, which means that the equine pupil should not be over-exercised at the age of three or four. In any case, short and frequent training sessions are preferable since they make less demand on the horse's limited concentration span than longer lessons.

The next important condition is that the horse should be fit enough to start its training. Lungeing is much more taxing for the horse than you might imagine: the continuous circling is demanding, and becomes even more so when the rider sits on the horse. I often feel that the horse is working harder than the trainer, which is both unfair and inefficient.

One particular experience, when I happily imagined that I was able to lunge a horse adequately and had passed my exams on this subject, taught me a lot about the effort ratio between horse and the trainer. I was rapidly disillusioned by a friend who was watching me.

'Do you call that lungeing?' I was asked.

'Yes,' I replied, 'What's wrong with what I'm doing?'

Without saying anything my friend, who had worked with E. Smit-Jensen, showed me not only how to work a horse effectively on the lunge, but also how hard I needed to concentrate. After five minutes I was exhausted, but it was an invaluable revelation. Smit-Jensen was a brilliant trainer of horses, and the indirect benefit of his techniques have made all the difference to my work with horses.

The effective trainer does not stand placidly, flicking the whip, while the horse makes all the effort, so if you intend training your own horse do seek out an expert to help you. Many riders think that putting on the tack and getting the horse to change pace and stop is all that is required, but this is only the first stage. Once the horse can go both ways on the lunge rein, obeying your commands, it is time to develop its muscles and propelling power in preparation for the rider's weight.

Talking Sense

Building communication with your horse is a profoundly moving experience. The resources that we use to cue the horse are the voice, gestures and contact signals, plus equipment such as the whip and spurs, which are really an extension of the signal given by the rider's legs. And we must not exclude the power of thought as a vital and empowering link with the horse. Call it telepathy or whatever you like, but non-verbal communication is an important part of the dialogue.

In order to reach this stage in communication, lessons must be built on the logical sequence of request–response–reward. This sounds simple to do, but it very seldom operates as it should, largely as a result of the trainer's delayed response, unawareness, or unrealistic expectations. When we request the horse to do something, the signal should be precise in order to avoid confusion. When the horse responds, the signal must cease at once. The cessation of the 'aid' or signal is in itself a reward. The horse soon learns the logic of doing what is asked, and the respite it receives for being obedient. The reward can be extended by saying 'Good', or patting the horse if you feel the response warrants further endorsement.

What often happens is that the rider asks the horse for something, then forgets to stop the signal when the horse is doing what has been asked. This is tantamount to a minor punishment, and can only result in confusion. It is important that the trainer notices the small gestures of willingness on the horse's part, and remembers to reward them. If this policy is adopted it will help to reduce the incidence of nagging riders who never stop kicking their horse's ribs. This is what I call the 'walk-on, walk-on syndrome', which can only result in the horse becoming physically and mentally numb to any signal from the rider.

Training Sequences

The majority of horses start their working lives without a sound basic education. People buy young horses without realizing what a risky step this is. Commercial

37

Some foals have more confidence.

pressures tend to push a horse on to the market as quickly as possible, and the animal may have had only a week's training in order to get it to accept a saddle and a rider. When you decide to buy, it can be extremely difficult to track down a well-schooled horse, and unless riding schools are lucky enough to find an old campaigner with some experience under its girth, they really need to train their own horses.

The training of a young horse takes months rather than weeks. Education can continue from one year to two or three, depending on the rider's goal. This time span can be compared with the length of our own education, from nursery and primary school right through to college or university. The equivalent of 'university' standard can be seen in the competition field, where some horses seem worthy of a doctorate.

There is really no excuse for horses not receiving a sound basic training, since there are many experienced trainers and good books on the subject. Commercial greed and ignorance explain why we still see so many unschooled horses struggling to carry riders. Not all horse dealers are exploiting the horse for the sake of their own pockets, but many do, and it is difficult for a novice buyer to see through the façade of good-looking but untrained horses.

THE SYLLABUS

So much depends on the horse's early association with its owner or owners. Horses that have been running semi-wild and are then rounded up for handling will find their change of environment from an open space to a stable quite terrifying. If this is followed by transportation to a dealer's yard, followed by a hasty introduction to a saddle and a rider, it can have a very detrimental effect. A temperamental horse may never completely recover.

If, however, the young horse is lucky enough to find itself in the care of someone with experience, its education will follow a very different pattern.

The nursery stage of training can start within a few days of birth, when the foal first has a headcollar put on and is gently encouraged to let itself be led alongside its mother. Some foals are much more confident than others, so great care should be taken not to frighten the more nervous ones. The foal should learn to be handled all over its body, to give it confidence in human beings. As the foal develops, words of command such as 'Over', 'Come', 'Walk' and 'Whoa' can be used. While it is young the foal learns, like a child, from listening to its parents. If used correctly, human language can augment the subtle equine one between the mare and her offspring.

Once the young horse is three years old the most serious part of its education can commence. So far we have been developing the horse's intellect by getting it to listen and pay attention to words, and learn obedience by producing the required action. Now it is time to begin developing the horse's body in readiness for the saddle and the rider's weight being placed on its back.

Leading in hand will now be extended to putting the horse round a circle on the lunge rein, where the horse obeys the same commands but at a greater distance. At first, you may need an assistant to stand on the outside of the horse in order to provide cue and control. It is surprising how quickly a good trainer can wean the horse from its reliance on the person who has been closest to it; they can soon be dispensed with, leaving the trainer with

A confident horse and rider.

Starting a circle.

Free, forward movement.

A change of scene.

full control. Walking, trotting and stopping can be taught in a few lessons, with the horse working equally and obediently in both directions. Working in a circle is harder than it looks, and requires the pushing power of the hind legs. As this power increases, the horse balances its body in relation to the circle, becoming both stronger and more supple.

I have not included the canter, because some young horses can find this difficult in such a tight area. Once the horse is moving freely forward, however, you can encourage greater activity by asking the horse to canter, at the same time being prepared to increase the circle by walking towards the horse as if extending the lunge rein. When you canter the horse you may well have to 'go walkabout' yourself so that it has more room. Some horses find the canter an easy pace; others have problems with it, and it is better left until they are ridden. In any case, too much cantering on the lunge places quite a strain on the young horse's joints. Free forward movement and calmness are the aims at this stage. If these can be achieved, the canter will develop when the time and place are right.

It takes between four and six weeks for a horse to reach a degree of fitness that will allow it to accept the weight of a saddle and rider on its back. This phase is referred to as 'backing'. When the transition has been accepted by the horse on the lunge, and it has learnt to obey the rider rather than the trainer, it is time to let horse and rider go solo.

The horse's balance can easily be disturbed during this stage of its training, and it is now the rider's aim to help it to adjust its centre of gravity by using its body differently. This can be done by encouraging the horse to engage its hind legs further under its body by using changes of pace, or transitions, variations of pace, and different permutations of loops and circles. Gradually the centre of gravity, which is over the withers when it is first ridden, will move back as the horse's quarters and back increase in strength. This process can take months. It is helped by riding the horse over undulating ground, and by varying the schooling environment to increase the horse's experience of the world and keep up its interest.

As in all aspects of education, calmness and patience are the keywords. Learning becomes impossible without them, and tension makes the horse stiff instead of supple. Free forward movement is the priority, with 'free' being the most important word.

You may feel that to implement these exercises successfully you will need a great deal of experience, but it is amazing what a sensible novice can achieve with adequate supervision.

4 Health and Happiness

We have seen how the dawn horse's natural habitat changed over the years, from the undergrowth where it browsed on leaves to the open prairies where it grazed on herbage. The horse managed to adapt to this changing habitat more successfully than many other species, and it is because of this ability to survive that this remarkable animal is still with us today.

The horse's world of wide open spaces shrank once human beings intervened in its life, gradually exchanging its natural existence for one where its speed and strength were harnessed to human ends, meaning ever-increasing restriction and confinement. The taming of the horse altered not only the horse's circum-stances, but also changed the course of our own history more significantly than many modern inventions.

This unique mammalian species deserves full recognition for the sacrifices it has had to make in the interests of human civilization. The best we can do to repay it is to take stock of its present role in our lives, and to recognize the conditions that are needed to make a domesticated horse's life a healthy and happy one.

The stable and the field are the two main living areas available to most horses, so we need to look at the advantages of each, being aware of the importance of space whenever we are caring for the horse.

42

The Stabled Horse

Any animal that is deprived of its natural liberty suffers some degree of stress. The horse is no exception, even after many decades of living in stables. The caged tiger will pound its den with compulsive restlessness, a restlessness which we can see in those horses who 'box-walk' their stables in the same way. We tend to take the horse's acceptance of the stable for granted, if only because so many horses appear contented and comfortable in this environment, but there are situations where this is not the case and the horse shows signs of distress.

We need to make certain that such situations are avoided, and to do this we must develop a better understanding of the horse and provide for its natural needs as far as possible. By putting ourselves in the horse's place, we can better see its point of view, and can implement constructive measures to improve the quality of its life.

When the horse is living in a stable, the following advantages will be apparent:

- The horse can be kept warm, dry and clean.
- It will thrive better on its food.
- It can therefore do more work.
- The horse is conveniently at hand when required.
- It can be clipped to make it more comfortable when performing fast work.
- It can be tamed or handled more easily.
- Its food and water intake, and passing of droppings and urine, can be monitored.
- Its general health can be kept under regular supervision.
- Its fitness can be built up, with a stable regime related to its food and exercise.

The stable itself needs to be:

- Large, airy and light.
- Well insulated and without draughts, since condensation from the roof often drips on to the horse.
- Large enough for the horse to have sufficient headroom, and space to lie down whether it is tied up in a stall or free in a loose box.

Other provisions of a horse-friendly stable include:

- Thick dry clean bedding.
- Regular, interesting exercise within the scope of the horse's ability.
- A constant supply of clean fresh water.
- A half-door over which it can look out.
- Protection from electrical appliances.
- A balanced diet.
- An opportunity to roll.
- Access to grazing and the freedom of the field.
- Regular grooming.
- Regular companionship.

When all these conditions are met, the stabled horse will be to some extent compensated for its unnatural confinement. To appreciate the importance of freedom to the horse, you have only to watch how it reacts, the joy it experiences, when it is liberated into a field after a winter spent indoors. It never seems to know what to do first: whether to gallop, graze, roll, stare at the surrounding country, or to whinny to a friend in the next field. This moment never loses its magic for me, and is one of the most precious moments of spring, reminding me of childhood holidays spent by the sea when I too found it hard to decide which of the pleasures I wanted to explore first.

Liberty.

Enjoying a roll.

Companionship.

The Horse at Grass

The alternative to stabling a horse is to keep it in a field, though it is wise to have access to some shelter should the horse become ill or injured. Grazing for horses needs just as much thought as stabling for them. To think that any area of grass will do is a mistake. Horses need more room than you think to obtain enough clean nourishment, ideally about two acres per horse. The fencing as well as the gate must be safe and secure, and poisonous weeds should be removed as far as possible.

Access to clean running water is very important. This can be supplied by a stream, if you are lucky enough to have an unpolluted one, providing it does not have a sandy bottom, because over a period of time the horse may ingest enough sand to cause colic. Ballcock-fed troughs that are protected from playful horses and have no sharp edges are a good source of supply, but do check them regularly. In winter they often freeze up, and in summer it is important to check that they are in working order and that the water pressure is adequate in dry weather. An old bath is not the answer; I once knew a horse who severed its tendons on the edge of one. Unfortunately not all fields are adjacent to a source of mains water, so water has to be carried to the horse. This is both hard work, and prone to human error: the horse can easily get an insufficient supply or the water can become stagnant. The horse that is short of water will dehydrate and begin to lose condition at once. A friend who owned a large number of horses could tell at a glance whether any of her horses had been short of water, and told me how easy it is for staff sometimes to miss a blocked water bowl or forget to fill an empty bucket.

45

Hidden dangers.

Domesticated horses are inclined to be accident-prone, so you need to foresee hazards such as the bath with sharp edges or a dangerous cast iron gate. I once saw a horse trap its leg in an iron gate in such a way that a hacksaw was needed to extricate it, an accident from which the horse never recovered. Horses are like children in their playfulness, and their confinement leaves them vulnerable to the dangerous objects with which we unwittingly surround them.

A safe water supply.

WORMS

Like the animal itself, the land on which you graze your horse needs rest periods and nourishment, so alternative accommodation will need to be found while this takes place. Overgrazing makes the field sour and worm-infested, creating sparse new growth, weedy with buttercups, docks and ragwort. You can help to slow this detrimental effect of grazing by picking up the droppings. You will still need to worm your horse very regularly in order to keep its worm count down to a tolerable level.

Except perhaps in specialized racing studs there is no such thing as a worm-free horse, because foals are born with an infestation from the mare. If we do not want to feed the worms instead of feeding the horse, it is our responsibility to keep this parasite in check.

Much research has been done on this subject, particularly by Professor Duncan of the University of Glasgow Veterinary School. He has proposed a much more rigorous worming regime than has previously been used: every six or eight weeks if the horse is at grass, rather than just twice a year. He has discovered that these parasites became resistant to the same remedy when it is used repeatedly, and therefore recommends changing the type of wormer used.

Worms not only cause debility and anaemia as they move through the horse's system, but also the blockage of blood vessels. These are called aneurisms, and they can sometimes have serious consequences, causing colic or even affecting the heart. Worming is a vital part of horse care, one which would not be necessary if the horse were free to roam large tracts of wild territory.

OTHER GRAZING CONSIDERATIONS

A horse out at grass in summer will require shade from the sun and shelter from flies and midges, the latter being as irritating to horses as they are to humans.

In the winter it will need shelter from the wind and rain: a three-sided construction in the field will provide this if there are no natural features that can fulfil this purpose. It is in these conditions that a stable can give the horse some welcome respite. Nothing pulls a horse down in condition as much as being constantly wet and cold, and it may be necessary to provide the horse with a waterproof rug to maintain its condition. In winter the horse will also require more feeding.

In the summer, on the other hand, feeding may need to be restricted, and the actual grass ration itself reduced. This applies particularly to those horses and ponies who tend to be overfat, and are prone to laminitis (also known as fever of

Poor land and fencing.

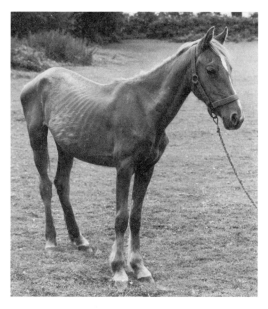

the feet). This is an extremely painful condition which can chronically impair the soundness of your horse, and can distort the shape of the feet if it becomes acute.

The horse's feet need regular inspection. A horse can easily cast or twist a shoe, and the nails can rise. If this happens on the inside of the foot the horse can cut the opposite leg. A horse will benefit from a period without shoes if you are going to rest it, providing the soles are not too sensitive or the walls too brittle. If you are in doubt about this, the blacksmith might advise putting on tips – just the toe of the shoe – to provide protection. This allows the rest of the frog to come to the ground as nature intended.

Always remember that a horse at grass is not as fit as a stabled horse, and you must not expect too much from it.

A case of neglect. (Photos: The British Horse Society.)

Eight months later on leaving the British Horse Society rescue and rehabilitation centre.

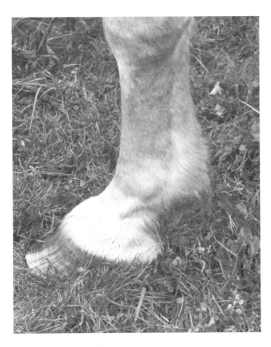

A foot distorted by laminitis.

Water

The important part that water plays in all our lives cannot be overemphasized. After all, our bodies are made up mostly of water, and horses are no different. The provision of water for the horse in the field has already been discussed; now we must look at how water can be provided when a horse is confined to a stable.

A horse drinks between 5 and 15 gallons (23 and 68 litres) of water a day, so if you multiply that by the number of horses you have, you may have to carry a lot of water daily. Probably the most labour-saving method of doing this is to use directly supplied water bowls, which should be placed safely in the loose box. Providing they are regularly supervised and cleaned, they can provide fresh water as the horse needs it. However, they can freeze up in winter, and there are some horses who never learn to use the sort that they have to press with their noses. The self-filling type are a much more satisfactory design. Like all machinery, water bowls are susceptible to malfunction. Another disadvantage is that the water intake of the horse cannot be assessed, and they are also expensive to install. You need to weigh up these points before you decide whether the time they save you is worth the initial outlay.

Buckets are the other alternative. They serve the purpose well enough if they are secured safely, kept clean, and refilled regularly. Keep them safely in a corner with the handle towards the wall. Sometimes it is necessary to keep two buckets with the horse overnight, especially if it has been exerting itself that day. It is much more natural for the horse to feed and drink from the ground, and it is easy to provide a removable container for food and to put its hay in a corner of the box, thus giving the horse the privilege of some natural behaviour as well as helping its posture. In this feeding and drinking position the horse's head and neck are lowered, and the muscles that you want it to develop when you ride it are brought into play, especially those of its back and loins.

Water need not be restricted except during fast work such as hunting, when only a few swallows during the day should be allowed. This will tide the horse over until its work is finished, when full access to water should be restored, although I think it is a good idea to take the chill off a bucket of water in very cold weather before a thirsty horse gulps it down. We all know the desperate thirst which follows a spell of hectic physical activity, and to be deprived of water when the body is crying out for it is quite unnecessary.

I have stressed the importance of water before the topic of diet, because all animals can live longer without food than without water. As a thirsty human being knows just as well as a thirsty horse, unassuaged thirst is torture.

The Horse's Diet

Even when a horse is stabled and fed intensively, it is important to keep its natural feeding pattern in mind. The wild horse roams, grazing more or less continually throughout the day, and its digestion is designed to cope with this lifestyle. The stomach is small and the intestines are large, which helps the horse to cope with the constant passing of fibrous grass through its digestive tract.

Horses do not spend their days eating grass and nothing else. They graze on virtually everything: bushes (even thorny ones such as gorse), herbs, weeds, barks, seeds, certain dirts and clays, and occasionally dung from other horses. I have even witnessed the disappearance of a 15ft-high mature tree – trunk, branches and leaves – all eaten within twenty-four hours! Why do they graze on such a variety of foodstuffs given the opportunity? The answer is simple: they intuitively seek a well-balanced diet. From grasses, leaves, seeds and flowers, weeds and herbs, barks, stems and other 'stringy' plant material, the horse obtains fibre, minerals and trace elements. Vitamins are obtained primarily from the leafy parts of trees and shrubs, fruits, and seeds when in season. Occasionally a horse might require some additional bacteria for its digestive system: this is obtained from the fresh faeces of other healthy horses.

When the horse is kept indoors it is

Ideal natural grazing.

difficult to simulate this process, but by feeding the horse little and often we can create a satisfactory compromise.

It is not natural for the horse to eat a concentrated diet, so the artificial food we give to it puts extra pressure on its digestion. One of the main afflictions caused by domestication is colic, which the horse avoided when in its wild state because it could select its own diet, knowing instinctively what was good for it. The secret of keeping its metabolism balanced is to provide bulk in the form of hay and chaff, mixed with the oats or other short feed. The amount of energy-giving food which the horse needs for its work must be balanced with the amount and type of exercise it is going to do. Bran is also an important regulator in the diet.

Foodstuffs for horses have changed just as they have for humans: we have all moved towards convenience meals. Until recently the old-fashioned ingredients of oats, barley, flaked maize, beans, molasses and linseed were made up into suitable feeds for individual horses. This meant that each horse was given exactly what it required.

This time-consuming process can now be replaced by complete food mixes or nuts, just like the ones available for cats and dogs. They are made up to provide the correct balance of proteins, carbohydrates and minerals for different types of horses and their work. You can buy racehorse, horse and pony, or stud nuts, according to your horse's needs. 'What could be easier?' you might think to yourself, and I agree that such foods have their place. Given the option, however, I like to

One method of damping hay.

make the horse's diet less boring, and more individually suited to that particular animal. In the wild, after all, the horse had a variety of grasses and other vegetation from which to choose, and not just the same old nuts day after day. Your horse may well have its say in this matter, refusing to eat what it finds unpalatable. On the other hand, the quality of nuts is consistent, whereas grains can vary with each new supply.

Something else that concerns me nowadays is the contamination that comes into the food chain, both from the soil itself and from the way that growing corn is sprayed with different chemicals. It is not easy to feed your horse organically, although I know of one small riding establishment which makes a valiant effort to do so by growing its own oats and making its own hay. I recall the days of making my own hay, in the days before we began to poison the land for the sake of production. It was hard work, and often a gamble with the weather, but the fragrant sweetness of meadow hay with all its wide variety of plants and grasses made it worth all the effort. I remember with less pleasure the first time I purchased oats that had been treated for mildew. This resulted in the oats' smelling sour and being unpalatable for the horses. I make these comments to provoke more thought about the present-day diet of the horse. There are plenty of mixes on the market, each making its own claims. My advice is to read the label carefully, ask as many questions as you can, and then try what makes the best sense to you and is acceptable to the horse.

Here are the basic feeding rules:

- Feed little and often, and do not work your horse for an hour and a half after feeding.

- Feed hay as bulk to replace the natural grass that your horse would normally eat.
- Make sure that hay and straw are not mouldy or dusty. To prevent coughing, some horses need it damped.
- Let the horse have access to water at all times.
- Feed only fresh, quality food.
- Keep food vermin-free.
- Let the horse eat in peace.
- Feed at regular intervals.
- Feed according to age, temperament and work.
- Feed according to your horse's metabolism; some thrive better than others.

More detailed information about the feeding of your horse can be obtained from the many good books on horse mastership which are now available.

Allergies

Insidious side-effects of diet and environment may undermine the immune system of horses, and I have a niggling concern about many of the allergies that some horses develop nowadays, and that I did not come across in my early days of horse ownership.

Horses that are fed too much energy-producing food without getting the exercise to go with it can suffer quite serious ill effects. These include azoturia, Monday morning disease, urea poisoning and laminitis. Some of these can be chronic and recurring. I lost a very special horse through incurable azoturia. The reason it developed this disease is still unclear because it never had a high oat ration in its feeds. The outcome was that its metabolism could not deal with the breakdown of protein. This affected its muscles so seriously that it became unusable at an early age, and had to be destroyed.

One mare that I was working with began shaking her head when at work. This habit persisted even in a headcollar, so it had nothing to do with the bit. At that time I was suffering from acute hay fever, which produced pain and irritation at the back of my nose. My vet was not amused when I suggested the horse's behaviour, with its sneezing and nose-rubbing, might be caused by a similar condition. Shortly afterwards I purchased a show pony who gradually developed the same problem; this too defeated veterinary diagnosis. In this state both animals became unsuitable for competitive work.

Then a student's horse began to exhibit similar symptoms. Luckily her father was a vet, so the three similar cases did produce some interest from him. My theory was considered, which resulted in trying antihistamine tablets in the horse's feed. This produced some positive results, but was an unsatisfactory way of treating the condition. The head-shaking remained a clinical mystery until, some time later, I met another case. This horse was being trained for dressage competitions, and its head-shaking made it difficult for it to compete. The owner decided to send her horse to the Dick Veterinary College in Edinburgh, where it was found to be allergic to flies and midges. The solution was to ride the horse with a fringe attached to the noseband, though even this led to only limited improvement.

The head-shaking must come from the irritation set up by flies, because the horses do seem very distressed while they are affected by them. My own mare used to keep putting her nose under my arm for protection.

Another problem is rain rash, which I do not remember seeing until well after the war. This affects horses that are out at grass, and appears in wet weather. They develop scabs that cover their backs, loins and necks, making them unfit to work if the rash is under the saddle or girth. The first time I saw it the outbreak appeared simultaneously in several adjacent localities, and I have seen the same thing happen several times since. Though the cause of rain rash is hard to pin down, it is thought to be an infection; I feel that it must have something to do with polluted rain water.

I am also concerned about the increased incidence of chronic allergic coughing in horses, caused by dust, which I do not remember experiencing with any of the horses I owned in the past. One cannot help wondering about these new symptoms from which the present-day horse seems to suffer, and to suspect that the undermining of the horse's immune system is caused by contaminants in the environment.

The Feet and Legs

LAMENESS

Even in the best-run stables the question of unsoundness can arise. Some horses seem to have a knack for getting into trouble. They can, for instance, lie down against the stable wall and be unable to get up (known as 'getting cast'). In the ensuing struggle to get to its feet, the horse may injure itself. There are also incidents of strained tendons and arthritic joints, as well as various infections.

It is worth studying diagrams of the horse's anatomy, so that you know where

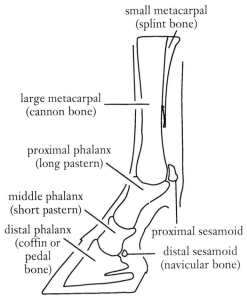

Bony anatomy of the lower limb.

small metacarpal
(splint bone)

large metacarpal
(cannon bone)

proximal phalanx
(long pastern)

middle phalanx
(short pastern)

distal phalanx
(coffin or
pedal
bone)

proximal sesamoid

distal sesamoid
(navicular bone)

ing, neglect or poor diet. There is an old adage which says that most lameness in horses arises below the knee. Swelling and lumps that appear on the legs and are caused by strain, bruising or splints are obvious, more so than the problems that may be hidden within the horn of the foot.

The remarkable construction of the horse's foot goes to show how clever nature is. The foot is the remaining toe of the horse's original five-toed ancestor, and evolved to provide protection and speed when it moved into the open prairie. Speed became the horse's primary means of defence – and still is – although when forced into a corner it will also use its teeth and feet as weapons.

The horse's foot consists of numerous blood vessels. The outer casing of the foot is called the horn or the wall. There is also an inner lining called the sensitive laminae. The foot grows down from the coronary band, which is clearly seen where it joins the leg and is very marked, when the foot is wet, as a white line under

the ligaments and tendons of the legs lie and can recognize the more vulnerable areas of your horse's body. The feet are often the culprits, as a result of poor shoe-

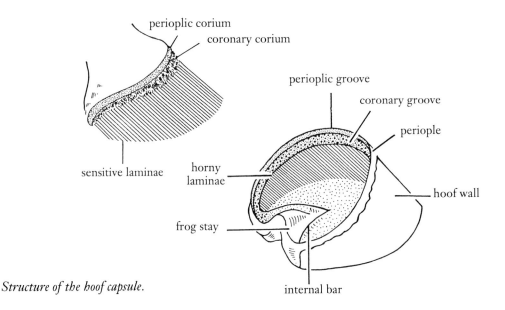

perioplic corium

coronary corium

perioplic groove

coronary groove

periople

sensitive laminae

horny
laminae

hoof wall

frog stay

internal bar

Structure of the hoof capsule.

the coronet. The laminae run down in vertical lines towards the sole. Here again the hard flaky sole has an inner sensitive sole which lies between the pedal bone, the navicular bones, and part of the short pastern bone which ends up below the coronary band. When the foot is lifted off the ground the joining of the wall to the sole will be clearly seen as a white line. This line tells the blacksmith where the sensitive laminae are, and is a guide to safe placing of nails when fitting a shoe. When a nail is piercing or pressing on this sensitive area it will result in lameness.

The bones of the foot are full of small holes, which make them porous and allow the blood to flow freely. They also make weight-bearing easier. The frog, which is a triangular shape, is positioned at the back of the sole, and acts like a pump as it makes contact with the ground, so that the blood supply is constantly being stimulated. The blood in the foot acts rather like water supporting a ship, and in this way the bones of the foot are cushioned and to some extent supported. If the frog is trimmed it will not make contact with the ground and its function will be reduced; as a result the foot will eventually change shape. As the frog acts both as a shock absorber and a non-slip device, it should be left as nature intended and not trimmed. Lack of frog pressure affects the heels of the horse, which contract inwards giving the horse's feet a narrow boxy look rather like a donkey.

The blood supply to the foot is crucial: too little can cause the foot to alter shape, and when frog pressure is absent the resulting jar that the foot suffers can lead to navicular and other problems; too much blood causes excruciating pain, and can lead to inflammation of the laminae (laminitis). Unlike soft tissue, the horn cannot expand, so the build-up of pressure in the foot can cause indescribable agony. This is one of the most serious afflictions from which the horse suffers as a result of its domestication.

SHOEING

It is not natural for a horse to wear shoes, but when humans started using the horse its feet began to wear away quicker than the horn could grow, making these protective measures necessary. The foot takes about nine months to grow from top to bottom. Shoeing a horse so that its feet are disturbed as little as possible is a great art. If too much horn is removed to make the foot fit the shoe, instead of making the shoe to fit the foot, the weight-bearing surface is changed. It also changes if the foot is allowed to grow too long, increasing the angulation of the joints and putting more strain on them. The same distortion is sometimes seen in dogs whose claws are allowed to grow too long. Horses also suffer from corns, which are as painful to them as they are to humans and come about for the same reason.

The nail-holes in the feet affect the horn by exposing this protective surface; as a result the horn becomes brittle. If a nail is driven too high it will come too close to the sensitive laminae, and may bruise them. It can also penetrate the laminae and set up inflammation. It is important to trot the horse out after it has been shod, and to be aware of any unlevelness in the next twenty-four hours.

The blacksmith has to contend with considerable difficulties apart from the basic problem of the horse resenting his attention – a perfectly natural response on the horse's part to an unfortunately necessary process. The quote about the battle

55

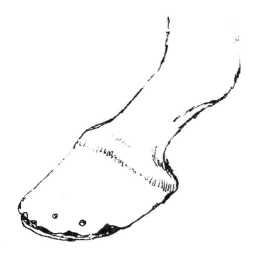

Overgrown foot.

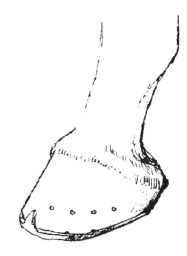

The same foot shod properly.

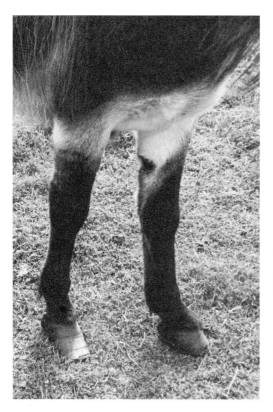

The neglected feet of a donkey.

being lost for the want of a nail is all too true. A skilful blacksmith can make a compromise with nature with the minimum of psychological and physical disturbance, and when bad shoeing or neglect has thrown the foot out of balance a good smith will employ remedial shoeing to redress the damage. This process takes time, because a drastic change to the shape of the foot can injure the sensitive parts and strain the joints.

Most horses will have some unpleasant memories of shoeing, because it takes patience and courage on the blacksmith's part to work with a young horse, or a frightened horse of any age. When a horse is being shod it too has to learn patience while it stands for an hour or more, first on one leg and then on the other, while the one being attended to is often held up at an unnatural and uncomfortable angle. The least we can do as horse owners is to prepare our horses for the blacksmith by simulating his sequences in the stable. If you cannot do this with your horse then you should not expect the blacksmith to do it for you. The same applies to the vet. It is important to train your horse to be obedient and confident in this way, so that a visit from either is accepted with co-operation. You should try to understand everyone's point of view in this situation.

It is a great pity when horses have to be twitched – held by a tight rope on the nose – or tranquillized in order to have its shoes put on. On the other hand, the horse's fear is just as understandable as the black-smith's anxiety about being injured. When deprived of the choice of flight, the alarmed horse will resort to fight. Then it will realize its own strength in the puny hands of humans. That horses seldom show this side of their nature demonstrates their ability to survive, tolerate and respect human intervention.

A horse's feet are often the key to that horse's happiness. When its feet hurt it cannot function properly. This is particularly true of horses with sensitive soles, animals which totter along apprehensively on rough ground; such horses would benefit enormously from having pads put in their shoes. Anyone who has suffered from blisters as a result of their own ill-fitting shoes will sympathize with the horse who is put in this position.

Symptoms of Stress

The next aspect of the horse's life which we need to consider is that of living alone instead of in a herd. There are still a few areas where horses do move in herds with relative freedom. The fell ponies I see on Shap Fell in the Lake District come to mind, as do the ponies of the New Forest, Exmoor and Dartmoor.

The horse that is deprived of contact with its own kind requires special consid-

Crib-biting.

eration. Although humans and horses have been together for thousands and thousands of years, there is a danger in taking its acquiescence for granted. There is abundant evidence to show that horses can live with apparent contentment and in good health without an equine companion, but a lone horse's excitement on those occasions when there is a get-together clearly demonstrates its pleasure in such company. If a horse lives by itself then its owner should not be surprised if it loses its head when it goes to a party. After all, many people do. How often have you heard the comment 'My horse is so excitable in company.' Why shouldn't it be overjoyed? To the horse it is a red-letter day, and when this happens you see your horse merely showing its natural instincts.

Some horses develop compulsive habits in the stable owing to boredom and loneliness: crib-biting, wind-sucking, weaving, chain-rattling, box-walking, and kicking the wall and box door repetitively. Once a horse develops one or more of these habits it is very difficult to stop it, and to prevent other horses in the same yard mimicking the behaviour. Wind-suckers arch their necks and swallow air, while crib-biters do the same thing while holding on to the edge of the manger or the box door. This results in the wearing down of the teeth, indigestion and flatulence. The weaving horse rocks from foreleg to foreleg, never resting. These horses tend not to thrive as

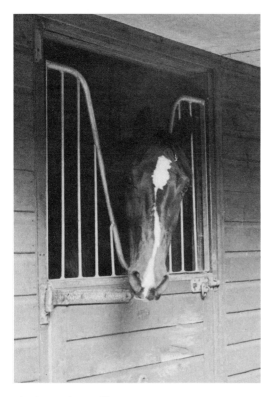

Anti-weaving grille.

well as their more tranquil counterparts, and put an undue strain on their joints and ligaments.

These idiosyncrasies are definite signs of stress, and any ploy that breaks up the monotonous hours of standing in the stable is worth implementing. One suggestion is to provide smaller hay nets more frequently, and to make sure the horse can look out of the box and see some activity, not just a blank wall. Two exercise sessions instead of one break up the day more interestingly, and so does a spell in the paddock if one is available. Some owners keep donkeys or even goats to keep their horses company if another horse is not feasible. In the past these problems arose less often because most horses spent their day working for their owners.

The main point is that you should be aware of the implications of solitary confinement, and realize that the horse must be compensated for its loss of liberty and equine companionship by having you as its leader and friend. I have known of the most endearing and enduring relationships, developing to the point where the horse in question was so well compensated that it resented the intrusion of another horse – or even a human being other than its owner – in what it considered its territory. It is particularly important to keep the natural horse in mind where young horses are concerned, because weaning time has its own traumas, and the play of foals and yearlings is part of a horse's natural education.

I know two schools in Scotland where horses live as herds, and I always find their behaviour fascinating. Rivalry, pecking order and friendship are a continual source of interest and information. There is no doubt that these two groups function and relate to each other and their owners

Playtime.

in a very different way from the individual horse. The exact difference is difficult to define, but I think it lies in the bond which unites the herd and includes the owner. We can supplement this natural socializing by intuiting the horse's needs. There are complications in being an 'only horse' just as there are in being an only child, and a word of warning: they can become just as spoilt!

Before this section on stress draws to a close I should like to comment on another, more insidious, stress factor which is connected with the horse's present-day environment: pollution. Those of you who keep horses at grass should check that the horse is not downwind when the next-door farmer is spraying his fields, while horses who live near busy roads may be exposed to excessive exhaust fumes from the traffic. Any of these pollutants can detract from the horse's overall well-being, its resistance to infection and its ability to tolerate stress.

Medication

Medical research has produced many very effective drugs, and surgeons have developed techniques which can repair torn tendons and set fractures which used to be fatal. The discovery of antibiotics is an example of how science has progressed. The Sulpha drugs saved the limbs and lives of many servicemen wounded during the Second World War, and I witnessed many miracles when I was nursing during the Dunkirk emergency.

When sulphanilamide was first available it seemed to be the answer to a prayer, yet the over-prescribing of the drug led to germs becoming resistant to it. Feeding it to animals in order to fatten them up more quickly exacerbated this trend, resulting in the need for stronger and stronger drugs to combat new strains of infection.

When antibiotic drugs are prescribed by the vet (or the doctor), the whole course should be administered. To stop half-way through because an animal or patient feels better is to precipitate this vicious circle of needing ever-stronger medicine. Medical practitioners know how much is needed to be taken for certain infections, and you would do well to heed their instructions.

I have recently been involved in such a situation concerning a dog belonging to a neighbour. A course of antibiotics was prescribed for its infection, but unfortunately the owner stopped giving the pills after a few days because the dog's condition had improved so much. Later the animal's problems recurred, and it took weeks of treatment before any real improvement was made.

The same principle applies when cortisone-based drugs are used. Stopping the treatment abruptly means the body has not had time to start manufacturing its own supply of cortisone. So when your horse needs treatment, do follow your veterinary surgeon's instructions to the letter. Your interference could make matters worse and, apart from the poor horse losing out, your pocket will also suffer.

Another emotive issue is the use of bute, an anti-inflammatory and pain-killing drug. The danger is that it can be used to make a horse workable when it is not really fit to work. If this happens, the original injury will usually be made worse.

To use a drug in this way is immoral, and only leads to greater suffering in the long run. Pain is, after all, nature's signal that something is wrong, and if we do not listen and use the advantage of modern treatment for the horse's benefit, we do the horse a great injustice.

Nursing the Sick Horse

Equine epidemics do occur, and spread rapidly as horses now travel greater distances to competitions. A horse suffering from an infectious condition should be isolated for the sake of other animals – not to do this is extremely inconsiderate.

If your horse appears off-colour, it needs rest, quiet, warmth, fresh air and a light diet. This means reducing the oat feeds and giving bran mashes with linseed, molasses or black treacle instead, and even a little grated carrot. Good old-fashioned nursing is still as important as medicine and, by helping nature to heal in this way, it can also reduce the side-effects which some drugs may produce.

The temptation to work a horse too soon after being ill or lame is sometimes difficult to resist, especially when important occasions are drawing near and modern drugs seem to make the horse feel better so rapidly. In the long run it pays to bide your time and to give your horse a chance to enjoy a period of recuperation after any setback. Rest is so often the best way of restoring health, because it allows natural healing to take place in its own good time. The horse is rather like the native tribes who were contaminated by contact with white people, for it is only when nature's laws are interrupted that epidemics occur. Both wild horses and native peoples living in their natural

60

environment are freer from disease than those who live in denser populations – one of the curses of civilization.

Education

Now that we have considered the various aspects of horse care, we have reached a point where its education becomes relevant. Education for the domesticated horse takes a very different form from that of its learning experience when running wild with its herd. When we humans take over the role of the senior herd leaders – the horses that would teach the young the elements of survival – we need to appreciate their function so that we can channel the horse's natural ability for our own use.

We must educate the horse so that we can exercise it safely and develop its usefulness in the direction to which it is most suited and most needed. No amount of feeding will improve a horse's health if it is unhappy doing what is required of it, so feeding and working are closely linked to the body/mind harmony of this once feral animal.

It goes without saying that a healthy horse will work better than one that is below par: it will have more resistance to disease and be less accident-prone. Its education can be built on this foundation of well-being, which improves both muscular development and mental composure.

Providing that the horse is not too young, the horse's education can make a promising start. At three years old the horse is ready for a gentle introduction to learning, and at four years, when it is stronger, it can accept a more progressive series of lessons. Horses do not stop growing until they are five years old, yet even after this I find that horses seem to go on

maturing each year if they are being fed and exercised in a happy environment. Examples of this year-by-year maturity of certain horses is demonstrated in star performers such as Red Rum and Desert Orchid, who gave of their best in their later years. Many of the more advanced horses in the Spanish riding schools are often doing their best work when in their teens.

Education means teaching your horse a language that comprises verbal commands and physical signals, which it is taught to obey. This training can be executed harshly, haphazardly, or logically and with understanding. The horse's relationship with people is affected for better or worse according to what it experiences during this process.

All horses benefit from elementary schooling principles which instil obedience and understanding, and which lead to physical changes in the horse: developed muscles and suppleness. At the very least it needs to be able to keep its balance with the rider on its back. This level of schooling prepares the horse for any specialized training to which its talents lend themselves. If, during this phase of its life, the horse's natural talents are directed in a sympathetic way, its potential can be channelled to achieve remarkable results. This sort of co-operation can complement the talents of the rider, too. With this level of mutual accord, there is a sense of growth which neither horse nor rider could have achieved without the other.

There is no doubt that some horses that have became famous for their high standard of competitive performance do sense the importance of these occasions, and experience the heady sense of success. You have only to see the winners of races and show classes to see how much the horses enjoy being in the public eye, and many of you will have experienced this with your own horses. Horses love pleasing their riders, but for this they need to be appreciated.

Pros and Cons

It is now time to draw some conclusions about the pros and cons of our domesticated horse's life, and to compare the main differences between the way they live naturally and the way most horses live today. Let us first consider the advantages of its natural habitat:

- Freedom to roam.
- A variety of pasture.
- Non-infected grazing.
- Room to gallop and play.
- Companionship.
- The security of having a leader.
- Not having to carry or pull weight.
- Not having to wear shoes, harness or bridles.
- Living in a family unit.
- Being less exposed to infection and disease.
- Grazing at dusk and early dawn, made possible by its good eyesight in the dark.
- Not being fenced in by dangerous wire nor being vulnerable to other domestic hazards.
- Natural mating.
- Rolling.
- Mutual grooming.
- Hardiness.

We can also look at the disadvantages of living naturally. These include:

- Predators.
- Injury with no medical attention.
- Shortage of food and water.

- Exposure to extreme weather conditions.

On balance it appears that the horse at large benefits enormously from nature's bounty, but is also at its mercy. The domesticated horse, on the other hand, has the following advantages if it is well looked after:

- Shelter.
- Warmth.
- Food.
- Water.
- Grooming.
- Fitness.
- Medical attention.
- Human companionship and affection, which can stimulate the horse's development beyond its normal capabilities.

The more I think about the horse's ability to serve human beings, the more I realize that this involves its living in unnatural conditions, and has done almost all the way through history. The ways in which horses have been treated in the past have often been harsh, cruel and even lethal. Yet against all its natural instincts the horse has allowed itself to be trained for many different purposes. Selective breeding has produced more suitable specimens for specialized work, and the temperament of the horse has changed as well as its physique. When people found that they were able to tame horses, the horse had to give up its natural way of life and become subject to a long list of restrictions and detrimental conditions:

- Physical confinement.
- Isolation.
- Cruelty.
- Hunger and thirst.
- Boredom.

Courtship.

- Fatigue.
- Lying in dung and urine.
- Injury and infection.
- Castration.
- Worm infestation.
- Selective mating.
- Shoeing.
- Clipping and trimming.
- Rugs and other unnatural clothing.
- Saddlery and harness.

There are many other things which could be added to these lists, but it will suffice to show that the modern horse has both gained and lost a very great deal. It has lost much of its toughness, its ability to endure extremes of climate and terrain. It is less resistant to ill health and stress. Certain breeds, the Thoroughbred being one of them, can no longer survive an outdoor life.

The horse has come a long way with us. We have changed each other, and although the disadvantages of civilization seem to outweigh the advantages, the horse has made its own remarkable evolutionary journey into the twentieth century. Many horses have accomplished great feats of endurance, prowess and courage in many parts of the world, and have done so for their human partners. Nothing ever stands still in nature, and the horse is one of its most progressive and successful examples of adaptation.

5 Grooming

Grooming plays a very important role in the successful management of any horse's welfare. It is one of the few real compensations we can offer to the domesticated horse for many of the freedoms we deny it. In this chapter, I include some grooming routines which form part of my students' training syllabus, and which you may not find in other books on this subject. I have done this because I have found them beneficial to the horse and, because they promote a more thoughtful and observant approach, to the groom as well.

You can of course incorporate your own ideas, and choose your priorities in the context of your particular stable

routine. If you follow my general advice, however, you will gain a fuller understanding of what is involved in grooming. Grooming is not just an isolated activity to promote physical health and fitness; it is also a significant part of the psychological welfare of the horse.

The natural horse can keep itself clean by rubbing, rolling and, if it is lucky enough to have a companion, mutual scratching. The stabled horse, however, does not have access to these facilities. In addition, the stabled horse will almost certainly be eating a more concentrated diet than its grazing counterpart; its metabolism will be working harder and

Mutual grooming.

exuding more waste material through the skin and internal organs.

A healthy horse is usually a clean one. The horse's coat is a barometer of its health: just like a human being, if a horse becomes debilitated, it is its hair that loses condition first. Even if it is living in a field, a healthy horse will have a bloom that is not present in the horse who has been undernourished or is in ill health. The horse in poor condition easily becomes infested with lice externally and worms internally.

It is often said that a good grooming is as good as a feed, and this is very true. The stimulation which this routine provides is a real tonic for the horse, helping its metabolism to function more effectively. This time spent with the horse becomes a special occasion for you both, and can be considered almost a mutual therapy, for no one can execute a good grooming session without being stimulated themselves. The better you become at it, the fitter both you and your horse will be.

Reasons for Grooming

Let us first look at the functions which grooming provides:

- It stimulates the circulatory system both of the horse and the groom.
- It removes mud, dried sweat, grease, loose hairs and scurf, enabling the pores of the skin and the sweat glands to function better.
- It improves the horse's overall appearance.
- It ensures that the feet and shoes are inspected regularly, and that a check is

kept on their soundness and health.

- It improves fitness, especially if a wisping session is included.
- Hand-grooming gives you a chance to observe any tender areas, swellings or other injuries.
- It provides an opportunity to educate the horse in stable manners and to increase your awareness and rapport with it.
- It helps to cement the friendship between you and your horse.
- It increases our knowledge of each horse's individual needs.

Strapping and Quartering

There are two types of grooming: the first is called strapping, and involves a thorough grooming; the second is referred to as quartering, and is a shortened version of strapping when the horse requires only a quick tidy-up. In well-run stables the horses will be strapped and quartered once each day. The horse's work will govern which way round these two activities are carried out. For instance, a police horse needs to look immaculate for its job, and will be strapped before it goes out to work, while the racehorse who is being exercised to make it fit benefits more from being quartered first and then strapped after its exertions have loosened the residual debris on the skin. The hunter needs to look its best at the meet and is far too tired to be strapped after a long day's work, so it will be strapped at the beginning of the day, and quartered on its arrival home to make it comfortable and to check for injuries.

Quartering the horse involves a quick brush over with a dandy brush or rubber curry-comb. If the horse is clipped out or is sensitive, this is done with a body brush to remove surface marks. The feet are picked out, and the eyes and dock are sponged. This is followed by a wipe-over with a stable rubber and a brief tidying up of the mane and tail with the body brush. The other expression for quartering, 'top tidy', describes the practicality of this form of grooming in making the horse presentable for its work. How presentable it needs to be depends on the role it is being asked to play, and whether it is stabled or not. It is not advisable to strap a horse who spends its life living in a field, and who needs the protection of the natural grease in the coat when the weather is wet and cold.

To do the job well you require the right tools, a safe place to work, and appropriate clothes to wear. No one can groom a horse thoroughly with their hair hanging over their eyes and floppy garments getting in the way. Bracelets, ear-rings, canvas shoes and sandals can all make you vulnerable. If you are not prepared to take your jacket off or roll up your sleeves, you are unlikely to get down to brass tacks. Even in cold weather I would suggest that you warm up in your sweater and then remove it as your temperature rises.

The professional grooms of the past could often be heard hissing quietly through their teeth, a soothing sibilant sound which the horses loved. The dexterity with which they performed the task and the immaculate results that appeared as if by magic exemplified this art.

Grooming Kit

Most people feel happier working with their own personally chosen grooming

Anticlockwise from top left:
metal mane comb; metal trimming comb;
plastic mane comb; metal trimming comb;
face brush with wooden back and nylon
bristles; round rubber face brush with nylon
bristles; pocket hoof pick; hoof picks.

Anticlockwise from top left:
wooden-backed, natural-bristle dandy brush;
plastic-backed, natural-bristle dandy brush;
wooden-backed, nylon-bristle dandy brush;
plastic-backed, nylon-bristle body brush;
wooden-backed, natural-bristle body brush;
leather-backed, natural-bristle body brush.

kit. It boosts the morale to have your own
equipment; tools which suit you quickly
become an extension of yourself. The following list of items should be included in
your grooming kit:

- Headcollar and halter shank.
- Spare bucket for warm water if this is
  available.
- Hoof pick.
- Small skip for catching muck removed
  from the feet.
- Dandy brush.

- Rubber, metal or plastic curry comb.
- Face brush.
- Water brush.
- Wisp.
- Massage pad.
- Stable rubber.
- Cotton wool or paper towels.
- Tail bandage.
- Mane comb for trimming.
- Hoof oil and brush.
- A box or bag for storage.
- A terry towel.

67

From top: wooden-backed, natural-bristle water brush; round leather massage pad; rubber groominh mitt with nylon bristles.

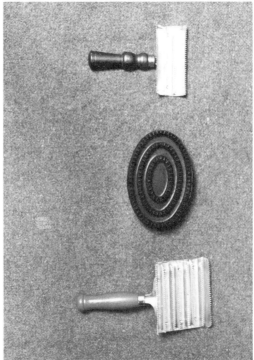

From top left:
small metal curry comb; oval rubber comb;
square metal curry comb.

- Brush, shovel and skip, for removal of droppings.
- Grooming mitt (optional).

Preparing the Stable for Grooming

The grooming session usually takes place in the stable, and careful preparation makes for efficiency. The stable should be clean and, if the floor is not slippery, you may prefer to keep the working area bare so that you can sweep it clean after the feet have been picked out or when droppings need removing. Water buckets should be removed for the sake of cleanliness, and the one you use for your grooming should be put safely in a corner until required. Tie up your horse to groom it, and teach it to move over and pick up its feet as required. The latter lesson will help the blacksmith. Do not let the horse push you about; encourage good behaviour by being firm if bossiness develops and calm when anxiety is present.

Grooming Procedure

Learning to groom efficiently means watching carefully how you use your time and energy. One of the first things you can usefully do is practise using both hands; in this way you will need to move around less and will have more room to work while remaining out of the kicking range of a ticklish horse. The stable should always be kept free of droppings while grooming is taking place.

Put on the horse's headcollar. A headcollar check is really part of the grooming process. It is important to see that it is adjusted correctly. I am surprised how often I see headcollars either drooping over the horse's nostrils so that they are almost falling off, or so big that a grazing horse could put its foot through it or get hung up on some protruding hazard. Make sure that the noseband fits where a cavesson noseband would be, roughly two fingers below the projecting cheekbone. Check that it is wide enough for the horse to move its jaws to eat, and for the throatlash to allow it to swallow. It should look neat but not restrictive; this is especially important when the horse is wearing a headcollar in the field. Tie up the horse with a halter shank clipped to the headcollar, and use a quick-release knot at the other end of the halter shank.

CLEANING THE FEET

Start the grooming session by cleaning the feet with the hoof pick. (A folding hoof pick is a useful item to keep in your pocket: should your horse pick up a stone in its foot when you are out riding, you will be prepared.) Check the horse's shoes for wear, looseness, and risen clenches (nails). Use a skip to catch the muck, or keep the floor bare until the task has been done, when you can sweep it up at once.

Stand by your horse's near shoulder, facing the direction of the horse's tail.

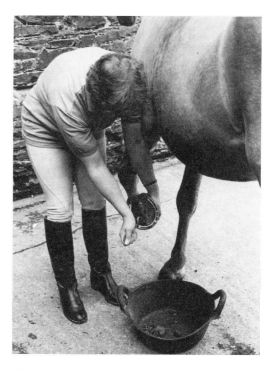

Picking out the feet on the near side. When picking out the feet on the off side, change hands and use the pick with the left hand.

Run your left hand down the near fore until you reach the fetlock, then pick up the foot as you push the horse's weight gently over on to its off fore. Support the hoof with your left hand, and pick it out with the hoof pick in your right hand. Do this from the heel towards the toe, to avoid poking the frog. Now move to the near hind and repeat the process. Reverse your hands on the off side of the horse so that you are working with your hands the opposite way round.

Finally, having checked each hoof and shoe when it was off the ground, check it again now it is on the floor. Remove the small skip, or sweep up the debris; then replace some bedding to prevent the horse from slipping.

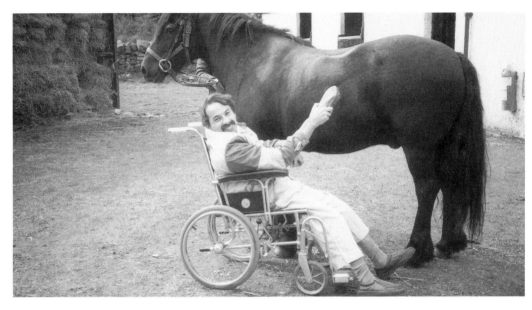

Ian using the dandy brush on Johnny. (Photo: Angela Stocks, Riding for the Disabled Association, Glenfarg Group.)

THE DANDY BRUSH

Using the dandy brush is the second step of your grooming regime. It has a wooden back and stiff bristles, which are now often made of nylon. It is used to remove mud and dried sweat on unclipped horses, and should only be used on the legs of sensitive animals. Stable or grass stains can be tackled at this point, but may need sponging to remove them. If you deal with them now and dry them off, you can brush them out later.

As with all brushes that are used on the horse's body, work down the near side of the horse's neck with your left hand and change to your right hand over its ribcage. Reverse this procedure on the other side. You can use this brush more liberally on horses who are out in the field and have thicker coats. Unlike the body brush, it does not remove so much of the grease in the coat, which acts as a waterproofing protection when the horse is living out of doors. The dandy brush is not suitable for the mane and tail.

THE BODY BRUSH AND CURRY-COMB

These two items are used together. The body brush has shorter and softer bristles than the dandy brush, and usually has a wooden back, though if you can find and afford a leather-backed one they are much lighter and more flexible to work with. This brush is used in a circular sweep, followed by some straight strokes. Put your weight well behind this action, and clean the brush with your curry-comb every three or four strokes. From time to time knock the dirt out of the curry-comb on to a bare section of the floor.

70

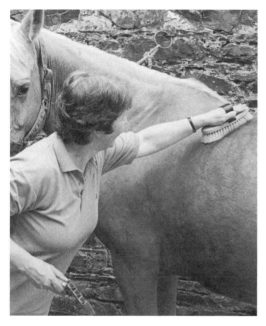

Using the body brush and curry-comb on the forehand.

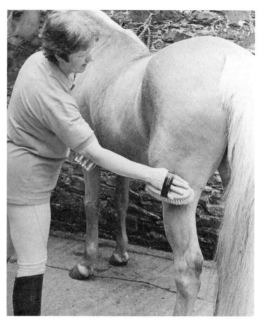

Changing hands for the quarters.

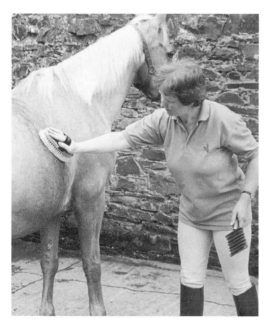

Reversing the hands on the off side.

Changing over to do the quarters.

As with the dandy brush, start on the near side of the horse's neck and work down towards its ribcage, then change over. You will soon begin to observe that your range of movement is improving, as is the strength in your hand and arm muscles. This will make for a more even feeling on the reins when you ride.

The body brush is more penetrating in its action, and removes grease, scurf and sweat from the horse's coat. Therefore, it should not be used on horses who live in the field. Use it to brush the head, and also the mane and tail as, unlike the dandy brush, it is unlikely to break the hair.

THE FACE BRUSH

The face brush is a recent innovation: a small bristled brush, slightly larger than a nail brush. This fits neatly into the user's hand as well as the awkward hollows of the horse's head, such as above its eyes or behind the jaw.

THE WISP

The wisp comes next, and is an item you will have to make. Start by making a rope of hay that is thick enough to hold in the palm of your hand with your fingers nearly closed. The aim is to make it the right size for your hand so that it is comfortable to hold. Wet the rope, and ask a friend to hold one end while you begin to twist the strands together. You need 6–8ft (1.8–2.5m), which will allow you to tie a knot and still have sufficient length at either end to thread through the middle until it is solid (*see* page 73). When it is completed, put it on the ground and jump on it to compress the strands and make it firm. Should your first attempt fall apart do not be discouraged; you will only improve your design with plenty of practice. What I have described is a basic design which I use myself; more elaborate designs can be found in other books, such as the manual published by the Pony Club.

The massage pad used like a wisp.

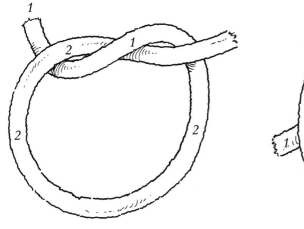

(a)

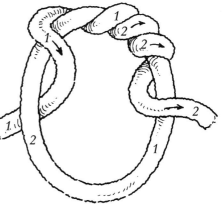

(b)

(c)

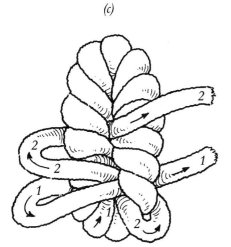

(d)

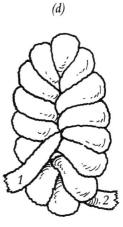

The wisp.
(a)   Start with a half-hitch.
(b)   Twist the ends around the loop formed by the half-hitch. Continue doing this until the loop is filled.
(c)   If necessary, for added security, push the ends backwards and forwards through the wisp, encircling each opposite side in turn. This will knit the two sides together.
(d)   Trim off ends as close to the wisp as possible, then place it on the floor and stamp on it to compact it.

73

The wisp provides a form of massage for the horse's main muscle groups, and is applied by raising your arm and letting its weight fall behind the swing as you make contact with the horse. This rhythmical swinging movement and the plopping noise the wisp makes as it touches the horse can become almost hypnotic. The horse's muscle tone is much improved by this routine, which should take ten to twenty minutes. The unfit horse may not tolerate too much firmness, but a fit one will be impervious to energetic wisping. In a sense wisping complements the exercise routine, and can replace it to some extent when enforced rest reduces physical activity.

I once found a home-made leather massage pad on a rubbish dump behind a smithy, which I used as a wisp. It was round and stuffed with horse hair, and had no doubt been used on the local Clydesdales.

Some present-day pads are made from synthetic materials, though leather ones are still available.

THE WATER BRUSH

The water brush is used to remove stains and to wash the horse's feet. It is also used to wet the mane in order to flatten the hair and make it lie neatly against the neck, and to wet the top of the tail prior to applying a tail bandage. Before this is done, however, it is as well to sponge the eyes, nose, lips and dock of the horse, using disposable material such as cotton wool or a paper towel.

Sponges are unhygienic for this purpose, especially when a number of different horses are kept. This routine may reveal the presence of worms, which show on the dock as white crusts.

HAND-GROOMING

You will develop a new insight into your horse if you hand-groom it before using the stable rubber (*see* below). Hand-grooming allows you to explore the ticklish areas of the flanks and up inside the hind legs, thus making sure the rest of the horse's body is clean. Your fingers can remove mud and sweat that the brush cannot reach. You may also discover a hidden injury. When you have done this you can be sure the horse has had a thorough going over and that all is well.

THE STABLE RUBBER

The stable rubber resembles a linen tea towel, and a tea towel can be used instead if you have a spare one. It is folded into a pad and used to give the horse a final polish to collect the surface dust left after the brushes have been used. Alternatively it can be used with the same swinging motion as the wisp, either when time is short or when a wisp is not available.

THE MANE AND TAIL

The material of the tail bandage clings to the dock of the horse, which is a difficult shape with which to contend, tapering as it does towards the bottom. Because this creates problems in keeping the bandage in place, there is a tendency to put it on too tight, and to tie the tapes at the bottom tighter than the rest of the bandage.

Careful attention is essential in gaining the expertise to lock each loop round the tail evenly, beginning at the top and continuing down the dock. White hairs that appear in lines on the tail are evidence that the circulation has been restricted at some time. When an overtight bandage is

Brushing the tail with the body brush.

removed and the circulation begins to re-cover, the horse may have to put up with more than we realize in terms of a numb tail and its after-effects.

The mane comb is a small metal comb about the size of a pocket comb. It is used more for pulling or trimming the mane and tail than it is for actual combing; using it for the latter can break the hair.

This brings us almost to the end of the grooming sequence, apart from oiling the horse's feet and grooming the tail. Excessive brushing of the tail, even with the body brush, can deprive the horse of this beautiful attribute by gradually reducing the amount of hair. If the tail is thick enough to brush with the body brush then hold the tail away from the horse and drop down a thin strand at a time until the whole tail has been done. Personally I prefer to use my fingers to tease out the tangles. If this proves too difficult, try washing the tail and then repeat the

Teasing the tail with the fingers.

teasing process. The difficulty can often be eliminated when the grease in the tail has been removed.

THE GROOMING MITT

The grooming mitt can be a useful addition to your equipment. It fits over the hand and is made of flexible plastic. One side is like a body brush, and the other is like a rubber curry-comb. People who have used it find that its flexibility makes it easier to groom the horse's head and other difficult areas of the body. The curry-comb side can be used instead of the dandy brush, and the hair which it collects is easily removed as it will fall out when it matts together. Some users have complained that it makes their hands sweat, but it can save both time and money.

At the end of grooming, leave the horse with a good bed where it feels safe to stale or to lie down. I have seen horses desperate to empty their bladders once they are taken out of the stable, where they have not dared to do so on the bare floor. Horses often lie down at intervals during the day, proving that to deprive them of bedding deprives them of valuable rest.

Treat your kit with care, wash it weekly, and it will last. Working with the right tools, tools which suit you, enhances the rewards of the process. Gradually your hands and eyes will become more aware of discrepancies such as heat in the leg, a tender back, a dull eye or altered respiration. These are the clues to which you will instantly react, and so perhaps be able to nip more serious developments In the bud. Good grooming is not only beneficial in the short term; it is also a good insurance policy.

At the end of a grooming session you too should feel physically exerted, and have a sense of satisfaction in a job well done and a relationship with your horse reinforced. This intimate time together has hidden benefits that put it into the class of a special therapy which you and your horse can share. How much better you will get to know one another in this environment may surprise you. As your awareness increases, you will make new discoveries about each other that could have far-reaching advantages.

Massage

I am convinced that the warmth of the hands can have a soothing effect on the horse's body. The hands held gently over any tenderness such as bruising may bring relief. The horse will soon tell you whether this contact is acceptable or not.

I once had an extraordinary experience with a well-known personality in the horse world and a pupil who bred ponies. We were debating the reason for the appearance of a hard lump, about the size of a walnut, which had appeared on the horse's back after work. The most obvious cause was the saddle. While we were talking my friend put her hand on the lump. When we turned to leave the stable I noticed that it had completely disappeared, and drew attention to the fact. Both my friend and the pupil were amazed. With a change of saddle the horse was able to work the next day.

REMEDIAL MASSAGE

Massage is the equivalent of an internal cleansing, stimulating the circulation and the lymph which helps the body to discard waste products in the muscles, so enabling

Finishing off with a brisk massage.

them to function properly. This is particularly significant for horses, who have residual tension in their posture when certain muscle groups remain tense and hard even when the horse is at rest. Massage may not fit into everyone's stable routine, but it does have considerable merit, as it can help to rehabilitate certain horses while they are at rest. It can develop your tactile appreciation of the horse's body and those muscle groups which need tone when the horse is being ridden.

There is a world of difference between the degree of tone needed by the horse to propel itself at liberty and that required when it has the weight of a rider on its back. The horse needs careful nurturing during its early schooling if it is to recapture its natural mobility, but far too many horses are deprived of the basic training which could make all the difference to

their confidence and capability to perform well. This deficiency can create unnecessary trauma and strain in the horse's early experience of being ridden.

If a horse becomes uncomfortable it will develop various evasions which affect the way it uses its body, and which result in a loss of balance. Dominant muscle groups that are needed for good deportment begin to deteriorate, while the opposite is true of those groups used by the horse to set up physical resistance.

The positive muscles, the ones that result from correct posture and balance, develop on the upper part of the horse's neck, giving it a strong elegant outline. This follows on down the back and the hindquarters, giving an impression of robust compactness which complements the arched look of the neck. These are not the only muscles that become prominent. The muscles on the inner side of the

77

thighs fill out, which is described as being 'well breeched up'. Observation of different horses will show that this is not always evident, and there can be a gap between the upper part of the hind legs when viewed from the rear, caused by poor condition or muscle tone. The horse's second thigh lies above its hock, and is another muscle that develops when the horse is properly engaging its hind legs.

The defensive muscle development occurs under the neck. The belly drops, the back and loins of the horse begin to look hollow, and the muscles over the hindquarters become flat with a pronounced croup. When this happens the horse's silhouette is reversed, changing from an elegant convex arch of neck, back and rounded quarters to a concave outline not unlike a sagging hammock, leaving the horse with a thick muscle under its neck, like a goitre, and a protruding belly as a result of lost abdominal muscle tone.

You can simulate this distorted posture yourself by hollowing your back while standing. This will result in your bottom sticking out and your abdomen being pushed forward. You can take the experience a stage further by doing the same thing when you are on all fours. You will notice your bottom will be up, and so will your head. The strain that this position imposes on you, as in the horse, can be increased by getting someone to press down on your back to simulate the weight of the rider. In this way you will begin to understand the mechanics of the horse's faulty deportment, and the mental stress which must accompany such strain and discomfort.

One of the first steps you can take to counteract this tense deportment is to feed the horse from the ground, which is after all what the horse does naturally. In this position the muscles on the top of its body, which have been contracted, are stretched, and the taut ones under the neck are relaxed. You can also check the height of the loose-box door. Small horses and ponies sometimes have difficulty trying to look out over them, thus encouraging faulty posture in another way.

You can do a great deal to help the horse to improve its performance without actually having to ride it, and having this back-up therapy which can take place comfortably indoors is of considerable value. An extra five or ten minutes spent with your horse in this way can work wonders. Touch has hidden benefits which we cannot always analyse.

HOW TO MASSAGE

The main thing that is involved in massage is becoming aware of the tone of the horse's muscles. Exert a tolerable kneading pressure in your work, and be aware of how the horse reacts. Some areas may be insensitive and others may be tender, so be tactful with your touch, and notice changes between sessions. A brisk tapping motion with the sides of your hands helps to tone the muscles by causing them to contract as you work on them. Let your hands be guided by intuition and the horse's response.

After you have completed the massage you can start to teach the horse a suppling exercise for its neck. Take the head and gently turn it in one direction a little way. Now release it for a few seconds before doing the same thing in the opposite direction. Very often you can tell at once, from the increased resistance you may feel in one direction, which is the horse's stiffer side. Be prepared for the horse having difficulty at first, because if its neck has been rigid it may want to turn its head by moving its hindquarters rather than by moving its neck.

The reactions displayed by the horse during massage provide useful information about the extent of its residual tension. If the horse is stiff in the stable, it will be even more so when it is ridden. Remember that muscles develop better if a rest precedes each new movement, because it gives the muscles time to recover after each effort. Also bear in mind that unaccustomed exercise can result in stiffness if it is overdone. Massage can help to remove the accumulation of lactic acid in the muscles, which can cause soreness and stiffness.

As the horse's back is particularly vulnerable, having supported the weight of the rider, you should check it regularly for any signs of tenderness. The hands can be used to dry off the sweat which is often seen under the saddle when it has been removed. A light patting movement of the hands can restore and stimulate the circulation in this area.

Breaking out is a term used to describe the cold sweat which occurs in some horses after they have been dried off after work. It is usually associated with excitement, exhaustion or anxiety. The patches usually occur on the shoulders and flanks of the horse, and its ears will be cold and clammy. When the horse is in this state it should be provided with a string rug and a light one to go on top of it. If the weather is warm the string rug will be adequate. If a string rug is not available, put a layer of hay or straw under a light rug to allow the air to circulate over the horse's body.

The use of your hands can be an effective way to get the horse dry. A gentle slapping movement of the hands will create warmth and relaxation. Pull the

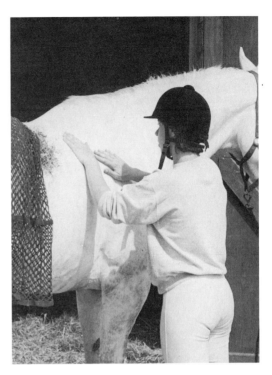

Drying off.

horse's ears gently until they too begin to feel warm. Horses that are prone to this type of nervous sweating may break out more than once before they finally settle down, so you will have to check your horse several times during the evening after strenuous or fretful exercise. Taking the horse for a walk is another way of helping it to relax.

Trimming

Although trimming the horse is not part of the daily grooming routine, I feel that a few comments should be made about the subject on the horse's behalf. Pulling out the hair of a horse's mane and tail in order to improve its appearance is at the least an

79

uncomfortable process, and often a very painful one. Plaiting, if done too often, can cause the hair to break, and plaits should be undone as soon as possible after an event. 'Hogging' is the complete removal of the mane, which should be avoided, while tail docking was made illegal in 1948. Fortunately Arabs and native ponies have always been exempt from these unnatural fashions, being considered 'correctly turned out' when in their natural state. Trimming the horse's heels at the back of the fetlock joint can expose the horse to cracked heels.

We would all be appalled if similar things were done to human beings, supposedly to improve their appearance, and horses should not be asked to suffer for the sake of fashion. We should always remember our responsibility to the horse, which cannot readily express a choice in the matter.

6 Equine Evasion

I was once asked to give a lecture on this subject. As I prepared my notes I realized that many problems that are attributed to the horse are in fact often caused by human error. Much to the surprise of the audience, I therefore changed the theme of my lecture to that of 'The Problem Rider'.

The Rider's Contribution

Troublesome behaviour on the horse's part is often a sign that all is not well with its environment, such as its housing, or with its physical condition; problems may also arise as a result of bitting, saddles, and training or work programmes. Bad riding can be another contributory fact, and this encompasses lack of knowledge and balance, both of which make life difficult for the horse. There are other factors, too, such as unrealistic expectations of yourself or the horse, and being in too much of a hurry. Some people are willing to lay out large amounts of capital on a horse, its upkeep and equipment, plus fees for tuition, but will then scrimp on the time required for the horse and themselves to practise. Not a few would-be riders have been known to put riding lessons at the end of their list of priorities, and taken tuition only after their relationship with their horse has collapsed. Time is a vital prerogative; you cannot buy it, you have to make it. When you create this breathing space, the development of awareness and fitness, and the assimilation of information and understanding between the two of you is made possible.

The Horse's Problems

Having said all this about the 'problem rider', the horse can be the culprit, sometimes as a result of hereditary factors which influence its mental stability or its physique. Physical defects, such as poor conformation, can limit performance just as a volatile temperament can result in unreliability. These traits can be handed down through the sire or dam, and are recognizable characteristics of certain parentage in one generation after another.

Another exception is the rare rogue horse, which can be the victim of heredity or of traumatic experience in human hands. We must also realize that pain can cause violent and unpredictable reactions in a horse. A brain tumour or an abscess on a tooth, for example, may cause the horse to be dangerous, rearing or running away without warning.

I have witnessed this sort of behaviour on three occasions. The first was a hunter with a history of running away. When he eventually had to be put down, the post mortem revealed a brain tumour. The second case had navicular in both feet. The third was a pony belonging to a pupil, which bolted without any warning and became highly dangerous. While the owners were deciding what to do, its nose began to discharge pus, so the vet was called. He discovered an abscess in the root of one of its teeth, which had infected the jawbone. This diagnosis finally resulted in the animal's humane destruction after treatment failed to produce a cure.

These examples show how carefully we have to observe our horses, and how much we have to learn in order to develop sound management and riding skills.

There is a saying that no horse is born bad – different, yes, and maybe with a difficult temperament and low stress tolerance, but not bad.

Understanding the Horse

The equine temperament is as diverse as our own, and is just as vulnerable to the more stressful aspects of the modern world as we are. When we consider its evolution through eons of time, place, climate and human intervention, the horse's ability to adapt to such traumas as noisy battle, loud traffic and supersonic aircraft, is nothing short of miraculous. In some ways horses seem to tolerate stress better than we humans do. When I taught at a Channel Island riding school adjacent to the airport, I was constantly distracted by the high-pitched noise of incoming and departing aircraft; the horses seemed to pay no attention to them at all. The same stolid reaction seems to occur when horses are exposed to low-flying fighter planes, which appear from nowhere with unbearable decibels of noise, leaving riders cringing while their horses remain calm. This poses an enigma about the horse's reputedly sensitive hearing.

The horse has unexpected reserves as well as unsuspected and irrational quirks and intolerances. I remember a splendid pony whose maturity and potential made it a perfect mount for his young owner, with whom he lived happily for a number of years. This pony was kept at livery and was used to being looked after by other people. One day a new student went to catch it in the field, and when she came back to say the pony would not be caught no one would believe her. It was eventually discovered that she had tried to grab its forelock, giving the pony a fright from which it never recovered its confidence. This pony had been broken in at the same stable, so its background was known to be a happy and confident one, yet this small error produced a remarkably dramatic change in this pony's behaviour.

Anomalies like these make the horse an intriguing partner. An animal's reaction to a particular person is significant, and even if we cannot always understand why they form their likes and dislikes or trust and mistrust, we should accept that they sense something which we are unable to pinpoint. If we work with animals then we must be prepared to accept their assessment of us, especially since, unlike ourselves, there is no malice in their opinions.

In normal circumstances a horse who is fortunate enough to find itself in good hands will have the chance to develop the physical strength to work and the mental confidence to enjoy it. When these conditions exist, the likelihood of problems arising is reduced. A knowledgeable owner will sense misunderstanding, fatigue, boredom, ill health and discomfort, and will make the necessary adjustments to eliminate the cause.

Unnatural Demands

We must remember that, even though it has done so for generations, the horse was not designed to carry or pull heavy weights. Selective breeding has produced different breeds for different purposes, but when we ride any breed of horse it puts considerable strain on its back, and is a physical impediment to its natural movement as well as a distraction to the horse's learning process. If you can imagine yourself in the horse's place, you might understand the implications of the pressure of an uncomfortable burden on your spine, and being expected to interpret signals that are often far from clear. Pressurizing a horse beyond its limits without a rest is quite purposeless.

It is essential to make time for learning processes to take place, and to accept that repetition of lessons is the only way to instil them.

I always remember an elderly gardener who was a source of sound common sense and much uncommon wisdom. His philosophy was such that he communicated equally with people, animals and plants. He seemed to sense the natural laws which influence growth and harmony. The result of this was a particular vitality which regenerated all who came in contact with him. He was often to be heard saying that you cannot force nature, or build Rome in a day. 'Give it time' was one of his favourite sayings. I often remember his example of quiet efficiency, working away contentedly in the garden.

Just as plants require a certain type of soil and location, so do different horses have their own particular needs. When the time comes for the horse to be educated, its physiological and psychological development will depend on the skill of its owner and trainer to appreciate what suits each individual animal, so that its full potential can be realized.

One of the horse's remarkable abilities is to be able to sense our own degree of attentiveness, being very quick to notice when we lose attention. On the other hand, it can also recognize a rider's absorption to such an extent that it too becomes involved, and starts to co-operate fully. This was demonstrated very clearly by one particular pony who had become sour and grumpy in his work, probably as a result of being over-exposed to competition stress as a working hunter pony. When he changed hands he was a very ungenerous and irritable animal, hellbent on avoiding work. Luckily for this pony it had found a caring owner, who took the trouble to understand what the pony was trying to tell her.

This period of assessment took some time, and for some time longer showed few results. The pony still lacked enthusiasm; if it felt a light tap of the whip it would buck, and would sometimes refuse to go forward at all when out on a ride.

Just as the patient owner was beginning to despair, a crisis arose because some photographs were urgently needed for a magazine. The pony was needed to help out, a rehearsal was arranged half an hour before the session began, and some intensive work was done to bring the pony's performance up to the required level.

Much to everyone's surprise the pony began to co-operate, and kept on doing its best throughout a long morning's work. When the session was finally over both the pony and the owner were quite transformed. For the first time since its arrival the pony was interested and friendly, and the owner was smiling happily because of its change of behaviour. Everyone involved had been intensely absorbed in the work required; it seemed as though this total concentration and commitment had caught the pony's attention and sustained it until the task was completed.

When demands like this arise, the horse can give us real food for thought. In this pony's case the transformation was quite remarkable. One can never be sure what takes place in a horse's mind, but this example certainly seems to offer evidence that some horses sense what is required and are able to rise to the occasion.

Fear and Resistance

A monotonous routine in the horse's training can be deadly boring for it. When schooling becomes a treadmill, there is a danger that some horses can become brainwashed. In a situation like this the horse's natural *joie de vivre* begins to wilt, and lethargy, resistance and restriction of movement become apparent.

When our expectations of the horse become unrealistic, we tend to fall into a negative way of thinking, which changes its relationship with us. Just as the horse can recognize the positive purposeful rider who is paying full attention to the task in hand, it is equally capable of recognizing the opposite. Relating is a two-way game, and no one plays it more accurately than the horse.

So-called bad behaviour in the horse is often its way of telling us that it is unhappy, and it is our responsibility to pick up the clues as to what the problem might be, such as badly fitting saddlery or shoes, tight bandages or a sore back. Since it is impossible to ask the horse what is wrong or where it hurts, we need to develop the faculty of acute observation, the extra sense which animals still possess and which we desperately need to redevelop in ourselves.

The horse is like a child in many respects, and there are close parallels between them where fear, panic and temper are concerned. It is all too easy to accuse the horse or child of mindless temper tantrums without understanding the fear which accompanies it; the borderline is very fine. Both need firm, calm, kind discipline, in order to give them a sense of security. The way in which horses react to fear can vary enormously. Some will present the equine equivalent of a temper tantrum, others will show resistance or paralysing panic. Resistance is a common defence when a horse is overcome by confusion; this type of panic is seldom recognized for what it is, and may result in the horse being punished for obstinacy.

The horse shows its reluctance to co-operate with its rider in a variety of ways. Here are some of the signs that your horse is not happy:

- Refusing to be mounted.
- Bucking.
- Refusing to move forward.
- Rearing.
- Running away.
- Pulling.
- Excitability.
- Shying.
- Being difficult to turn in one direction.
- Napping back to the stable or field gate.
- Refusing to jump, or running out.
- Kicking.
- Biting.
- Refusing to be tied up.
- Wind-sucking.
- Crib-biting.
- Box-walking.
- Tearing rugs.
- Refusing to be caught.
- Threatening to kick when cornered.
- Pulling back on the halter rope and getting away.
- Being aggressive with other horses.
- Jumping out of the field.

Some of these problems have their roots in poor conditions and training; others are related to anxiety and self-defence. We need to find the reasons behind the horse's protest so that common sense and logical discipline can give the horse a sense of direction and a chance to do its best. Tracing the origins of the horse's behaviour in its unnatural environment is like being a detective, because what happened to it in the past may be difficult to unravel. On the other hand, the nature of the horse's undesirable behaviour may be the clue to the cause.

When you buy a horse you also buy the results of its previous owner's treatment of it. Finding a horse from a good background, which suits your temperament and ability, is far from easy. It is well worth while taking your time over the decision, listening both to a reliable person's advice and your own intuition. Remember that when a horse changes hands, everything in its life is turned inside out, and it needs time to adjust to its new home, new diet and new owners. One riding school I know well allows its horses a month to become acclimatized. Horses travelling to a new country will need even longer to become acclimatized to their new home, even if the journey is comparatively short (such as it is from Ireland to mainland Britain).

Most minor difficulties can be resolved fairly quickly, so it is the more limiting and threatening exhibitions of disobedience that we need to look at in more detail.

BUCKING

Bucking can be triggered by the same factors that make a horse refuse to be mounted: badly fitting sadlery, or a sore back. These reasons are much more common than any lack of training on the horse's part. Once the rider is dislodged the horse finds release from its pain, and will naturally try it again. Some horses have cold tense backs, and are prone to hump them when ridden forward after being mounted, giving the rider the

Bucking.

impression that they are about to buck. It can be helpful to lunge a horse that tends to buck so that it can warm up and relax its back before being ridden. I believe in lunging any horse that has been laid off work to avoid this particular habit, as it prevents an unexpected fall for the unwary rider. Once you are mounted, try to keep the horse's head up and ride forward energetically in trot, on a circle. Another option is to walk round on a small circle, which will divert the horse's attention and put it in a position unconducive to bucking. Riders soon learn to recognize this taut feeling in the horse's back, and the difference when it relaxes. Some horses will buck when going into canter, so be warned and keep a firm control on the reins. Having said all this, the habit can be caused by no more than *joie de vivre* and overfreshness.

NAPPING

When a horse refuses to go forward at the rider's request, it can be for a number of reasons, some of which are more serious than others. The horse may have become insensitive to the rider's leg, or has not understood what is being asked of it, or has been kicked so much it has stopped trying. It could be unwell, bored or tired.

This difficulty can be particularly irritating to the rider, and shows the importance of free forward movement in the horse's training. The answer does not usually lie in using more leg; instead you need to use your brain, showing the horse how to respond to a polite request from the rider. However, if a horse stops dead when it is out for a ride and refuses to go any further, it can produce a confrontation which is difficult to resolve. This behaviour is called 'napping'. A horse can also nap on seeing a jump, refusing point blank to go any further. This generally arises from too much jumping, which disheartens the horse, or from the rider's interference with the horse's balance. The horse that naps on the road or towards the gate in a field is obviously anxious to go home, and may be objecting to being alone.

Extreme fear may be the underlying cause of this difficulty. More basic schooling can help, during which the horse learns general obedience. Sometimes it helps to get off and lead the horse forward;

Napping.

at other times this simply rewards the horse. You can try turning the horse on a tight circle to keep it moving; since this manoeuvre is uncomfortable it may decide that walking forward is preferable. Another tactic is to allow the horse to stand until it becomes fed up. This could take a long time; you might begin to feel hungry, but so will the horse! Riding with a companion may give the horse confidence and help to break the habit.

I can relate a recent success story about an old pony who napped consistently whenever his new owner tried to go for a ride. She decided to reschool him in spite of his age. Much patience was needed to give the pony time to develop his mind and body, but as his school work improved the napping habit was eventually cured.

REARING

Rearing, like napping, can be very difficult to resolve; the rider's feelings of fear and helplessness add to the dilemma. Both napping and rearing involve the complete cessation of the horse's forward momentum, and it is important to check out all possible causes for this resistance, particularly bitting and teeth. Every technique I have tried is unpredictable in its results, and often the danger that rearing presents is not worth the risk of trying to find an immediate solution.

Horses at liberty will sometimes rear in play or in a show of authority over the herd. However, when the horse rears with a weight on its back, the rider's loss of balance can result in the horse being pulled over backwards. This of course can cause injury to both the rider and the horse. On the other hand, if both escape unscathed, the fright may stop the horse repeating this form of resistance.

Rearing.

I once bought a young pony from the Channel Islands, knowing it had started to be very disobedient through lack of training. The first time I lunged it the pony reared repeatedly. I decided that if I could manage it, the best tactic would be to unbalance the pony as it went up in the air. When I did so, the pony was very surprised to find itself on the ground. It never reared again, and proved to be a willing and talented pupil. I think that this pony was a natural herd leader who had found in her first contact with human beings that she could manipulate them in this way.

While we must always consider the contribution of a heavy-handed rider or a painful bit towards a habit like rearing, there may also be more deep-seated physical or hereditary causes. Whatever the causes, however, a rearing horse is a serious liability. Should you ever be caught in this situation, remember that it is more difficult for the horse to rear if its head is to one side. Hold on to the mane to keep your balance.

RUNNING AWAY

The tendency in a horse to run away can be very dangerous, because once it is in full flight its state of panic can make it impervious to the rider's attempts to gain control. Being on a runaway horse is a very frightening experience, especially since it can happen unexpectedly and for no obvious reason. Even though the reason may not be obvious, however, a reason there must be. Rapid flight is the horse's natural defence in a hostile situation and, when you consider what we ask of many horses, it is surprising that so few of them do bolt.

A horse that pulls can make its rider feel that their control is being eroded, but the difference between this and running away is quite distinct. The runaway horse will tend to have a moment's aberration, where control hangs in the balance, and if you are unable to make a rapid decision to turn it on to a circle it will be too late and the horse will quickly gather speed.

I recall an occasion when I found myself in this predicament on a pupil's new horse. Luckily I sensed what was about to happen as the horse stiffened its body, and managed to turn it and stay in control, but it was a near thing. I discovered later that the horse had a history of 'taking off' in this way. Fortunately its rider was experienced enough to be able to do what I had done, and as a result of reschooling and re-bitting it became quite successful in dressage competitions. I suspect the trouble arose in its previous jumping career, because it became much more unmanageable in that environment.

PULLING

A pulling horse is one with an uneducated mouth, or a mouth that has become deadened by severe bitting, and which has lacked good basic training to improve its balance. Pulling often develops through insensitive riding and rough hands, with the result that the horse's weight is always on its forehand. This wheelbarrow momentum makes it difficult for it to stop, even when it wishes to do so. The rider struggles for control and ends up holding the horse up, so that both partners find themselves in an escalating tug of war.

If the horse's mouth has not become damaged then basic schooling and kinder bitting will usually reduce the problem. The horse has a natural tendency to resist the feeling exerted on the reins when it does not understand what to do. When the horse is taught how to respond with softness through yielding to a signal from the rider's hands, it can understand the signal better and the tiring resistance can be reduced. The horse's progress will depend on a rider who sits in a balanced position, and whose hands are sensitive to the most vulnerable part of the horse's body. The horse's mouth is in your hands. The combination of sensitive hand and leg signals helps the horse to balance itself by placing the hind legs further underneath its body. It is then able to move its centre of gravity further back, and in doing so begins to counteract the heaviness of its shoulders which makes it difficult for it to stop or slow down.

EXCITABILITY

Some horses are more volatile than others, and highly strung animals can pose problems for the inexperienced rider.

This temperament is reflected in the horse's body language, which changes dramatically when the horse becomes excited, exposing it to damaging postural distortion. Examples of this behaviour can regularly be seen on the racecourse and at showjumping competitions. Such horses tend to evade the bit by carrying their heads too high. The back is then forced to hollow, which in turn prevents the horse from bringing its hind legs underneath its body. When this type of horse is controlled by too much rein action its pent-up energy can force it to leap into the air off all four legs. The horse literally explodes in desperation. This habit can be called fly jumping.

These horses suffer enormous discomfort and even pain, which may well lead to later unsoundness. They are difficult to keep in top condition, and to ride. Their behaviour creates a vicious circle, because the rider's reaction to it is often illogical. Coming to terms with these sensitive animals depends on the restoration of calmness in their lives, so that they can learn to relax not only at work, but also when they are at rest.

While the rider feels forced to control the horse entirely on the reins because they dare not touch it with their legs, progress is impossible. To believe that taking your foot off the accelerator altogether will slow the horse down is erroneous. The horse feels insecure and does not know why, and must learn to accept this connection with the rider. Introduce this new sensation to the horse on a small circle, so that the horse can be kept under control while it learns to accept that your legs are now part of its body. The circle will help to calm the horse so that the rein contact can be adjusted to the horse's tolerance and your ability to maintain

Physical distortions caused by the horse's tension and the rider's heavy hands.

contact. After the horse's initial surprise at these tactics, it will suddenly begin to relax. Its whole demeanour will start to change, and its head will come down. These horses are probably the most interesting and rewarding to work with, providing you have the skill and the patience. They are often highly intelligent, willing to please, and have enormous courage and endurance. When the breakthrough comes it is worth all the time you have spent in calming it down.

Remember to reward the horse for every attempt to lower its head, and allow it the freedom to explore this new experience. It may become excessively demanding in this respect, but this phase will pass and provide the opportunity to build up the horse's deficient muscle groups by doing some of your work on a long rein.

SHYING

Shying is another way in which the horse's natural fear is demonstrated. This instinct, like running away, is still roused in

Shying.

certain situations, even after many millions of evolutionary years. This is the natural horse coming to the surface when it feels threatened.

Some horses are much more persistent shyers than others, to the extent that it becomes a major disruption, and in a dressage test it is penalized. I have much sympathy for these horses, because in most cases their fear is genuine and is only increased by the rider's irritation and aggression. This sort of behaviour on the rider's part shows that they do not really understand what the horse is trying to tell them. How often do you say that your horse is doing it on purpose, or that it is being silly? What the rider fails to appreciate is the horse's instinctive fear response, and how much they add to this by their own negative attitude.

When a horse shies, the rider is usually caught off guard, losing both mental and physical equilibrium. Less experienced riders may well feel that they might fall off if the movement of the horse is a violent one, and any rider is justified in having an anxious moment if the horse shies in front of oncoming traffic.

To understand why horses shy is the first step in dealing with this behaviour. Most often a horse shies because an object on its path looks unfamiliar in shape and colour. The horse may not recognize colour in the same way that we do, but it is thought to see some colours more easily than others, and to be affected by sharp contrast in light and shade. If this is so, the horse may experience something we see as harmless as threateningly lifelike. In its primeval state, such an object might have been a predator. When this happens persistently in the same place we are apt to condemn the animal for stupidity, forgetting that the imagined terror will change continually according to the way the light falls upon it. The horse's eyes focus differently to our eyes, requiring the head to be positioned at a certain level for it to focus effectively. This is something we do not always allow the horse to do.

The best way I have found for dealing with shying is the technique of 'non-resistance', as used in the martial arts. This is more effective than forcing the horse up to whatever is causing it fear. This jostling only compounds the horse's anxiety, and the rider becomes an extension of the horse's object of distrust.

The technique of non-resistance works by using the rider's awareness and a single point of attention. The key is to keep your mind occupied and interested. The relaxation that results from the exercise reduces the tension which has built up between you and the horse. When force is reduced, a calmer situation is allowed to take the place of resistance. Obviously you cannot put this technique into practice on a busy road, but as the horse can shy in the field or in a schooling arena, an opportunity may arise where it can be tested safely.

A second option is to work the horse at a distance from the trouble spot. In a field or a school, it might prove possible to ride within three or four yards of the obstacle that is causing difficulties. You can experiment with the distance while learning to sense the tension building up in the horse.

You may be surprised to find the horse gradually becoming acclimatized to whatever was frightening it. In most cases distraction is far more effective than attack. It is always worth dismounting and leading the horse up to its *bête noir*e. This will help young horses in particular, who feel reassured by smelling and examining strange objects.

An example of shying happened recently in a lesson which I was taking. The horse in question had a reputation for being excitable, but proved to have more of a problem with violent episodes of shying. The rider tended to blame the horse and to become irritated by its evasions, and felt they must be repressed. When insistence failed to produce any useful results, I suggested a change of policy. This produced good results on one rein, but less improvement on the other. Having exchanged annoyance for interest, the rider decided that this was probably due to some stiffness on that side of its body. As the exercises proceeded, the horse became calmer and less inclined to shy.

Heredity

The following story illustrates the influence of hereditary factors, and demonstrates how these can influence the way horses may behave with different owners.

After the war some New Forest ponies were being crossed with better-class Thoroughbreds. At intervals the youngsters came up for sale, and one of them arrived in my own locality. I first saw this four-year-old mare out hunting, where she was behaving impeccably with a young rider. She continued to conduct herself with exemplary behaviour throughout the season, and was even willing to allow her rider to close gates while everyone else galloped off.

When the season was over, her owner decided to train her for show-jumping. During this time something traumatic must have happened, which upset the pony so badly that she not only refused to jump at all, but began retaliating by rearing when punished. This behaviour led to even more severe and delayed reprisals; these were totally illogical and eventually made her impossible to handle. She continued to rear and fall back on top of riders who tried to cure her.

Knowing her history, I purchased this pony to give her a chance in a better environment. It took a very long time for this beautiful pony to feel sufficiently confident to proceed on all four legs, instead of constantly rearing on her two hind ones. The animal had become terrified of going forward because she was so afraid of the conflicting bit and whip. This constant panic meant that the pony had lost all communication with her trainer.

In due course, some improvement was made by riding the pony in a soft rawhide bit, and sometimes only a headcollar. With a quiet and tactful rider, she managed to cope with a little light work.

Thinking about what might have happened, there is a possibility that this pony damaged her back during one of the confrontations before I bought her. As she was not entirely reliable, and the work she could tolerate limited, I decided to breed from her, feeling that the pony's temperament was basically good and that rough handling had unhinged it. She proved to be a good mother, producing a very attractive filly which we broke without any problems at all. She was just as docile as her dam had been at the same stage. A friend of mine liked her so much that I was persuaded to let her buy the pony for her own children to ride.

Some years passed, during which I lost touch with both friend and pony. Then I heard that this pony had won a championship under another owner's name. The new owners happened to be clients of mine, so I contacted them to offer my congratulations and to find out how they had acquired the pony. They told me a sad story about how they had seen her at a

sale, and because she was so thin they had felt compelled to rescue her. Luckily for the pony, she had fallen into good hands. That same season, however, the husband died and the pony was put on the market again. I tried to buy her back, but unsuccessfully, since the judge who had awarded the championship had already acquired her. As it happened I also knew the judge, but I did not press the point and the pony went north.

More years passed before the pony and I crossed paths again. She had by this time moved on to another home, but the new owner had become ill and asked me if I would look after the pony temporarily. I was, of course, delighted to do so, but then I discovered to my horror that she had become nearly as delinquent as her mother, though in a different way. She was a delightful pony to ride, but once I was off her back she became antisocial. She was reluctant to be caught in the field or the loose box, and exhibited very threatening defensive behaviour if I persisted. She showed every sign of being a dreadfully unhappy pony who had lost all faith in humanity. In spite of all my efforts to bridge the void between us, I never did make friends with her again. She returned to her owner and then moved yet again to other acquaintances, where she continued to lead her lonely depressed life.

I never knew what eventually became of her, which saddens me to this day, but I did realize that somewhere in her hereditary make-up there was a low tolerance to stress.

Both mother and daughter had had unfortunate experiences in their lives, from which neither of them recovered, whereas other horses seem to have a resilience which restores their goodwill whenever kindness prevails. I believe that the

This pony's tail shows resistance going into canter.

Overfresh horse serpenting the tail.

A relaxed tail.

daughter had a foal herself, and I often wonder what hereditary traits displayed themselves in her offspring. Did they come from the original New Forest pony or the Thoroughbred sire? There was at least a happy ending to the dam's story: she was sold to a loving family wanting a brood-mare, and settled down most successfully in her new home, where she lived happily to the end of her days. Both these stories tell us something about the horse's long and indelible memory.

Tell Tails

The way in which a horse carries its tail can tell us a great deal about its moods. The mannerisms displayed can be a warning to the rider that misbehaviour is imminent. As the rider cannot see the tail of the horse, they need to sense the accompanying tension that can build up in its back. When the horse swishes its tail fussily from side to side you can almost hear it saying, 'If you come too close, I will kick.' The horse shows its frame of mind by using its tail in other ways, too. The horse that bucks often clamps its tail tightly against its buttocks. Some horses produce a kink in the dock which is called a serpent tail: this can indicate that the horse is feeling above itself. When the tail is carried to one side it can be a sign that the horse is feeling stiff; it can be helpful to lunge such a horse with its saddle on before riding it. This will give it time to warm up and let off steam, and allow the trainer a chance to observe its body language. The tail of a relaxed horse swings gently from side to side in time with the tempo of its paces.

I will end this chapter by making reference to that famous horse Granat, who performed so successfully during his life with Christine Stukelberger. His death in 1989 must have been a deep grief to her after experiencing such a special partnership with this great horse. Granat was tremendously strong-minded, as well as having unusual gymnastic strength, and was at times so volatile that he was almost uncontrollable. This is a classic example of a working partnership at the highest levels of the dressage world. Its attributes were so unique that the horse's outbursts were an accepted part of the relationship. As Christine Stukelberger discovered, dealing with a 'difficult' horse is a question of building up a working partnership that is based on mutual understanding and trust.

7 Bits and Pieces

Early domestication of the horse would have required some form of restraining equipment, and it is interesting to conjecture what this might have been, and what materials would have been used. American Indians probably used a rope or leather halter, or a loop of rope round the horse's lower jaw, and rode bareback. Before the wheel, horse haulage would have required sledges, and when using horses as pack animals the load would have needed securing. I have a hunch that the earliest horse breakers were well-attuned to all aspects of nature, and would have had the ability to control the horse on intuitive levels that we may have forgotten.

By the time of the Romans, the horse was more evolved and harness had become more elaborate. The snaffle, which had been in use for a thousand years or more, was now made of metal. Horseshoes also appeared, needed because the horse's work wore the horn of the foot down more rapidly than the rate of its growth. This is a classic example of human interference with the natural horse. Shoes, however well-fitting, are an unnatural device which weights the foot and penetrates the horn with nail-holes, making it brittle and sometimes causing corns and bruising.

The Right Bit

The bit is another unnatural impediment which the domesticated horse has had to endure over the centuries. Horse owners should understand the purposes of the different bits and the action they have on the horse's sensitive mouth, jaws and poll, so that horses can be ridden safely and in comfort.

There is an old saying that there is a key to every horse's mouth, a particular bit to suit an individual horse. In order to find a suitable bit for a particular horse, we should take advantage of the wide range available to us. The introduction of a foreign body into the horse's mouth should be made as natural and painless as possible. Because this sensitive part of the horse's anatomy is also where other discomforts manifest themselves, we must not assume that all bitting problems are mouth-orientated. For example, a horse can become very fussy about the head and mouth when it is in fact stiff in its back or hind legs, or resents the way it is being ridden.

It is essential to have some information about the variety of bits you can buy before choosing one for your particular horse. You must also understand the anatomy of the mouth and jaw. The horse's mouth is a curiously long shape, and the lower jaw is much narrower than many people realize. The narrowest part of the jaw is at the gap between the incisor teeth at the front of the mouth and the molars at the back. The bare gums at this point are called the bars. The bars are vulnerable to injury because the jawbone is sharp, and the gums have little protection apart from the skin which covers them. A gelding has four extra teeth which lie behind the corner incisors of the lower jaw; these are called tushes.

The tongue forms a soft barrier upon which the bit should lie comfortably, providing it is not too heavy. Some horses find this pressure on the tongue intoler-able, and try to evade it by pushing the tongue over the top of the bit, thus exposing the bars of the mouth to direct pressure and often resulting in bruising. This problem can be a difficult one to resolve, but a careful choice of bit may help to break the habit.

Differences in the construction and proportions of individual horse's mouths can be very considerable. Externally, the lips of some horses are coarser and thicker than others, and when viewed from the side the depth of the mouth itself also varies. A horse with a shallow mouth will have less room to accommodate a bit, and so a thinner one will obviously be required. Internally there are other variations. If the molars in the lower and upper jaw are so sharp that they are cutting the inside of the cheek and the tongue, the teeth will need filing before a bit is introduced. Another problem is that of 'wolf teeth', which, although small in size, are often an irritant. These can easily be removed by the vet. Occasionally horses develop an abscess on a tooth, and can also suffer from a build-up of tartar which, though not a major disaster, is unhealthy and makes the breath unpleasant. Inflammation of the gums can occur when food is impacted in crevices in the mouth. Always ensure that the horse's mouth is clear and healthy before a bit is fitted, so that it will fit comfortably and cause no irritation.

A bit takes up space in a horse's mouth. How well the horse tolerates this intrusion will depend to a large extent on the proportion of the mouth and the tongue. If the tongue is rather thick and long and the bars too narrow, or the roof of the mouth is puffy, there will be too little space for a bit, and this will cause excessive pressure on the tongue. On the other hand, if the tongue is too small the bars will be exposed to pressure, which may lead to bruising.

No bit will produce the desired control unless the horse is taught how to respond to pressure on its mouth. The horse's initial reaction can be flight or fight if bitting is not done with great care and proper knowledge. The horse's mouth is extraordinarily sensitive, and it surprises me that it tolerates this impediment at all.

If your horse has an insensitive dry mouth, a mobile bit may help it to become more responsive. You may have heard the saying that a wet mouth is a soft mouth, and wondered why this is so. Perhaps you can relate this syndrome to your own dry mouth when you are under stress. In general a wet mouth is a sign of relaxation, allowing the saliva to flow. On the other hand, you do not want your horse frothing and foaming as it champs the bit. This is a sign of agitation, and the sooner you find the cause the better. Try changing the bit to a more rigid or thicker type.

Bits are mechanical devices that help us to control and direct the horse, and any bit, however mild, can be severe when the rider is heavy-handed. Do not forget that there are people who are able to ride a horse without a bridle: Shuna Mardon was a good example of someone with this ability. She rode her horse Strathdon in cross-country competitions with only a neck strap. This demonstrates that the horse's performance depends not so much on the bit as on the education and fitness of the horse and the skill and tact of the rider.

Types of Bit

The various types of bit that have been designed through the ages are countless, since each era saw a range of new inventions with which to control the horse. The severity of some of these prototypes was quite extreme; not only was excessive pain inflicted, but severe damage was often caused to the horse's mouth tissue and jawbone.

When I sat my professional exams before the Second World War, candidates were expected to be well informed about a wide range of bits. I spent much time and considerable anxiety trying to remember all the names and actions of as many different types as possible. This situation has changed considerably, and today far more emphasis is placed upon understanding the permutations of the snaffle, rather than on knowing about obscure bits named after their inventors. It helps to remember that there are three main types of bit, each one representing a particular principle and action:

1. The snaffle, which has a single mouthpiece and one rein;
2. The pelham, which has a single mouthpiece and two reins;
3. The double bridle, which has two bits and a separate rein for each.

In the past, before other metal amalgams were discovered which were easier to keep clean, most bits were made of hand-forged steel. These amalgams – nickel, eglantine and vulcanite – are still in use. The breakthrough of stainless steel provided the best of both worlds, being both strong and easy to clean. It is some time since I have seen chromium-plated bits in use, which is a relief, since they often resulted in flakes of chromium being ingested by the horse. Cheap thin nickel bits crack at the edges, and wear at the place where the rings go through the mouthpiece, causing sharp edges dangerously near to the corners of the horse's mouth. Thin bits are more severe, and in the hands of a rough or unbalanced rider can be like pieces of wire in the horse's mouth. Other available materials to consider using are glassfibre and even rawhide, which can be used for young horses with sensitive mouths. Rawhide was used successfully at Temple House where I did my training with Major Faudel Phillips.

The material used for a particular bit will govern its weight, temperature and texture. Steel, for example, is very cold, while vulcanite feels warmer. I often wonder how we would like to have a lump of ice-cold metal thrust into our mouths on frosty mornings. You can show consideration for the horse by warming the bit in your hand as you carry the bridle to the stable.

THE SNAFFLE

The snaffle bit has been in use since Roman times. It is interesting because of the varying action it can have on the horse's mouth. The most common version now in use is probably the jointed snaffle, which acts more on the corners of the mouth than on the bars, and has an upward nutcracker action. The jointed snaffle has various permutations, such as the loose-ring or eggbutt snaffle. The joint of this type of bit lies in the middle, so that it forms a 'V' in the horse's mouth. Because the joint provides a degree of mobility, tongue pressure is minimal, but it is important to ensure that the bit fits the shape of your horse's mouth, not only matching the width but also the depth from the front to the corners. When the snaffle is too wide it either dangles down in the mouth with the point of the 'V' near the

incisors (or the tushes of a gelding), which invites the horse to put its tongue over the top of it, or, if adjusted to compensate for this, the horse's mouth is pinched in the 'V'. The only remedy for these problems is to change the bit for one that fits. A horse with a sensitive mouth, who tends to fidget with its bit, requires quite a rigid design, while a horse whose mouth seems insensitive needs more mobility. The mobility of the bit depends on whether the rings on the mouthpiece are loose, or welded on.

If the bit is to act on the mouth correctly, the horse's head must be carried in the correct position, with the head flexed at the poll and the face slightly forward of perpendicular. If the horse raises its head,

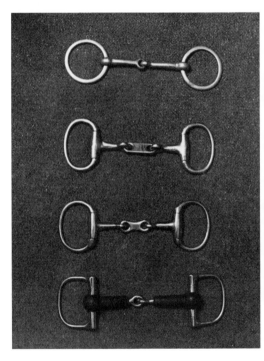

From top: loose-ring snaffle; Dr Bristol; French bridoon; D-ring jointed vulcanite snaffle.

the angle of the action is altered, causing the bit to act severely on the corners of the mouth. Resistance to the bit distorts its effect, as can be seen in the illustrations on page 89.

Some snaffles have two joints instead of one, such as the French bridoon, a useful bit with a small butterfly-shaped link in the middle which turns the shape of the bit as it lies in the mouth into a 'U' shape rather than the usual 'V'. When used correctly, this reduces the nutcracker action and makes it a milder bit. An important advantage of this more mobile bit is that its use is permitted in dressage competitions, unlike the Dr Bristol. The main difference between the two is the longer, flatter link in the middle of the Dr Bristol, which makes it more severe. Another less common two-jointed snaffle, called the 'W'-mouth snaffle, has two thin mouthpieces, each with offset joints on opposite sides. This bit is more severe on the mouth, and is an exception to the one-mouthpiece design of the snaffle group.

Choosing a Snaffle

When deciding which bit will suit your horse, consider the effect you want it to produce. Think carefully about whether the bit you choose will solve any problems: for instance, if your horse pulls, consider the possibility that it is caused by lack of schooling rather than a bitting problem. Remember that no bit on its own is going to produce miraculous results unless the horse is trained, well-ridden and in good health. The success of any bit lies ultimately in the skill and tact with which the rider uses the reins, and this in turn depends on the rider's ability to ride in balance without using the reins for support. This is referred to as having 'an independent seat'.

A change of bit during the horse's education can often be a good idea. Until you try something new you will never know whether it will work. If a change would be advantageous, your horse will probably give you the clues.

Take note of the available space in your horse's mouth, as some horses' mouths are simply too small to accommodate a thick chunk of metal, even though a thicker bit is usually a kinder one. A heavy bit creates more tongue and poll pressure, so if you want a thicker bit without compromising lightness, you could buy a German snaffle, which is hollow.

If your horse dislikes the jointed snaffle, make sure that the molars are not

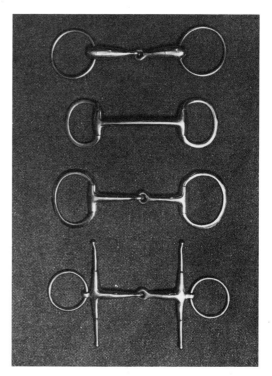

From top: German snaffle; eggbutt half-moon snaffle; jointed eggbutt snaffle; Fulmer snaffle.

99

sharp and cutting into its cheek where the rings of the bit press on the outside. Some horses simply do not like a jointed snaffle, but will happily accept a straight bar or half-moon version which acts on the bars of the mouth rather than on the corners. However, these bits do not give the same sense of finesse when steering the horse, because the bit, being rather like a rigid pole in the mouth, is affected at one end by any pressure exerted on the other. This is less likely to occur with a jointed bit, because each side of it is independent. You may well have to compromise, at least in the short term, until further training or greater fitness makes a change of mouthpiece possible. Another disadvantage of straighter bits is that their mild action can cause horses to 'lean' on them, causing the rider to feel that the horse's head is being held up by the reins. When this happens it is time to try a bit that is more mobile, and less likely to encourage the horse to support itself on the rider's hands.

The Fulmer snaffle is another option. The advantage of this bit, with the cheekpieces incorporated in front of the rings, lies in the way in which it reduces the nutcracker action of the jointed snaffle. The cheekpieces of the bit are fastened on to the bridle (*see* illustration on page 107) which lifts the bit up into the horse's mouth, making the 'V' shape less acute. This bit is usually made with quite a thick mouthpiece which, coupled with its modified action, is kind to the horse. Being a stable bit, it discourages the horse from champing on it and becoming unsteady with its head. It cannot be pulled through the mouth like a ring snaffle and, as it acts more on the bars than on the corners of the mouth, it is a useful bit for a horse that tends to carry its head too high. Because the bit is quite heavy, it increases the pressure on the poll, encouraging the horse to lower its head. The rigidity of the Fulmer snaffle may make some horses feel wooden and, because it is mild, some horses may begin to lean on it.

Less common, but useful for horses with sensitive mouths, is a jointed vulcanite snaffle. I have found that it works very well on young or sensitive horses.

Fitting

It is important to fit jointed snaffle bits correctly, but this is not always easy to accomplish when often the only sizes available are full, cob or pony. Full-size bits are far too wide for most horses, and it is usually best to borrow different sizes before buying in order to get the width exactly right. As I have said, horses have narrower mouths than many owners realize, and often a pony bit is wide enough. The bit needs to be stable in the mouth, otherwise it will move too much, either sliding from side to side or banging up and down and bruising the bars. On the other hand, a bit that is raised too high will drag on the corners of the mouth and place excessive pressure on the horse's poll.

To check the fitting of a jointed snaffle, gently open the horse's mouth at the side where the bars lie, and with a finger pull the joint down the tongue to see where it lies when the horse is not holding it up with its tongue or teeth. If it is too low, you will find the apex is near the front teeth. Another check is to lift the rings to see if the cheekpieces of the bridle bulge. If they do, the bit is too low.

Here is a full checklist for fitting a jointed snaffle:

- Check that the bit is the correct width.
- Check the way the bit lies in the horse's mouth and on its tongue. The bit should

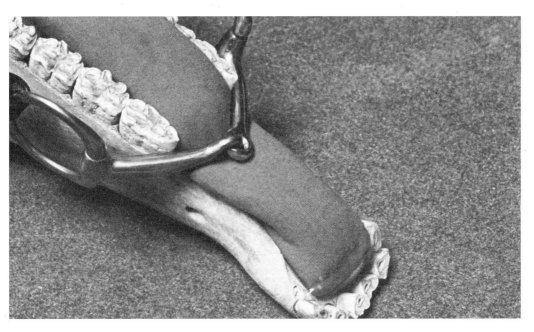

The bit is too wide and too high.

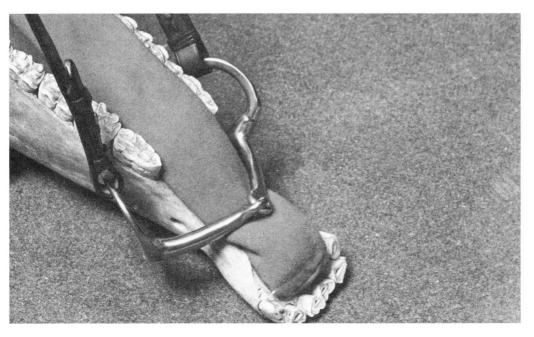

The bit is too wide and too low.

101

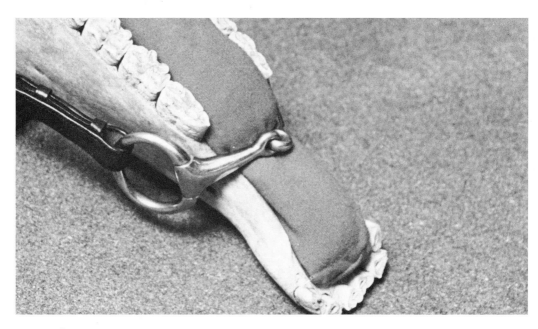

Correct fitting.

be fitted closely into the corners of the mouth without dragging them up uncomfortably or increasing the poll pressure.

- Check the pressure at the poll by putting a finger under the bridle.
- Check the condition and smoothness of the bit, making sure there are no blemishes in the metal that could cut or tear your horse's mouth.
- Check the horse's response in relation to its balance, fitness, and standard of training and riding.
- Be aware of any behavioural changes or the development of bad habits.

THE PELHAM

Pelham bits have one mouthpiece, but two reins (*see* illustration on page 103). They are not as popular as they used to be, perhaps because they are not allowed in dressage competitions. It is easy to reject a bit that might be described as unfashionable without considering its pros and cons.

The Pelham is made up of a straight or half-moon mouthpiece, a curb-chain and a cheekpiece on either side, to which the reins are attached one above the other. The top rein is the snaffle rein, and its action is that of a straight bar snaffle; it is therefore mild because it acts on the tongue and bars without pinching. The second rein is attached to the bottom ring of the cheekpiece, and acts like a lever on the curb-chain, which is fitted behind the jaw in the chin groove. The longer the cheekpiece, the more severe this action becomes, and this is why these bits tend to be used on horses who are difficult to control. The leverage affects the pressure on the poll and compresses the jaw, so that a horse can find itself trapped between this

102

pressure and that of the curb-chain. This will lower the horse's head. Some horses will flex the jaw when they feel this, which results in the nose moving towards the chest.

Some Pelhams have a slight arch, called a tongue groove, which counteracts this problem by allowing more space for the tongue. A pronounced arch in the middle of the bit is called a 'port', and should be fitted with great care. If it is too high it can damage the roof of the mouth. The jointed Pelham is a severe mixture of jointed snaffle and curb-bit leverage, and has little to recommend it.

Nowadays the most common Pelham has short cheeks and, if the curb-chain is fitted correctly, it operates only when the bottom cheekpiece is pulled back at an angle of 45 degrees to the perpendicular. It is reasonably kind to the horse, yet greatly increases the rider's mechanical control. This makes it a useful bit for children on strong ponies. As children have difficulty holding two reins, let alone keeping an eye on their individual tension, a small loop is fitted which combines the two rein actions into one. This gadget is known as a 'Pelham rounding'.

The main disadvantage of the Pelham is that the two rein actions cannot be used individually. The overall effect of the bit is thus somewhat contradictory, as one action effectively cancels out the other.

Show ponies are often seen wearing Pelhams, because although the double bridle is in fact the correct turnout in the ring, children and their ponies can find these difficult to cope with. One of the most popular Pelhams is the vulcanite Pelham, with its short cheekpieces and warm thick half-moon mouthpiece.

My personal feeling about the Pelham is that it is a rather unsatisfactory amal-gam of snaffle and double bridle, without the benefits of either. However, there are occasions when it is useful, for example when playing polo, for which the rider needs instantaneous control while holding the reins in one hand. In most cases the Pelham should be regarded as a temporary solution.

DOUBLE BRIDLES

The third family of bits is the double bridle. Here we have two bits, each with its own rein, so each can be used independently. This is a much more complex piece of equipment, and should not be

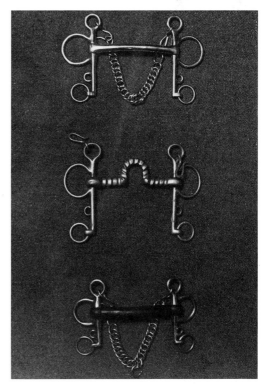

From top: half-moon Pelham; severe Pelham with high port and grooves on mouthpiece; vulcanite Pelham.

used until the horse is mature enough to benefit from its use. An example of this standard is seen in the Spanish Riding School and in advanced dressage horses. Think of the double bridle as a rather special prop which adds real finesse to an actor's already talented performance.

The two bits are fitted one above the other in the horse's mouth (*see* below). The jointed snaffle, or bridoon, lies on top, and has an upward influence on the horse's head. The 'bit', as the lower one is called, lies just below it. This is straight with a tongue groove or port, and incorporates a curb-chain. Both the chain and the cheekpieces are similar to those of the Pelham, and the same considerations apply regarding its severity. However, with the double bridle it is possible for the rider to adjust the reins so that they ride mainly on the bridoon, only using the bottom rein when the flexing of the horse's head and lower jaw is required.

This bridle can be used inappropriately if knowledge and skill are lacking, and if the horse is too young. Although the double bridle is part of the traditional turn-out in the show ring and the hunting field, horses are more frequently seen hunting in milder bits, and young show horses are often introduced to the ring in simple snaffle bridles.

The double bridle takes up a lot of space in the horse's mouth, so it is important that the horse has confidence in the rider's hands and is willing to go forward freely. Its balance and carriage must be fully developed, or it will become over-bent and restricted in its paces.

There are three types of double bridle, the difference between them lying in the design of the bottom bit:

1. The Weymouth has the cheekpiece slotted through a hole in the mouthpiece, which gives it slight mobility;
2. The Banbury has the mouthpiece slotted through the cheekpiece, which allows

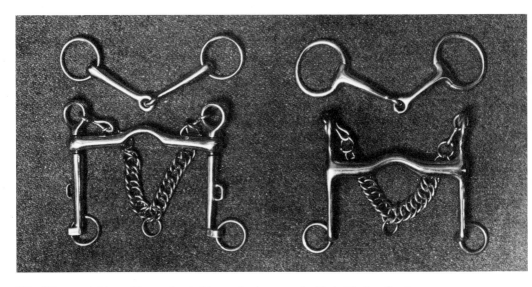

The Weymouth bit and loose-ring bridoon; the dressage double bridle has fixed cheekpieces and eggbutt bridoon.

the horse to move it up and down with its tongue;

3. The fixed cheek has the mouthpiece and cheekpiece welded together, making it rigid.

The Weymouth was once the most commonly used, but more recently the fixed cheek has come to the fore. The Banbury has lost some ground, probably because its mobility creates problems with the horses mouthing it too much, though I have always felt it was quite a gentle introduction to a mouthful of ironmongery.

THE BITLESS BRIDLE

The bitless bridle may seem a more humane way of controlling the horse, but if

The bosal hackamore.

it is not fitted and used correctly it too can injure the horse's mouth, although the damage may not be so evident.

The English hackamore, with its metal cheekpieces, works on a lever principle like the Pelham and double bridle, but exerts its pressure on the nasal bone, curb groove and poll instead of on the mouth. As the cheekpieces are quite long the effect can be severe, and it is not a bridle for the uninitiated. This bridle is designed for Western riding, where the horse is taught to obey neck reining. Riding in the English way with this bridle is limited. If you try to use a hackamore in the English way of riding, you will find it very difficult to steer your horse. If you must use one, find an experienced Western rider to fit it for you, and show you how to use it correctly. I have seen the inside of horses' cheeks cut to ribbons by riders using the reins as if the horse was wearing an ordinary bridle. The term 'hackamore' comes from the Spanish word for nosepiece.

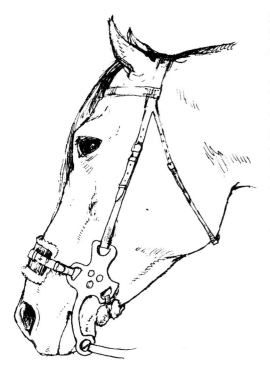

The English hackamore or bitless bridle.

The bosal hackamore is a bitless bridle with a firm noseband; it sometimes has two knots which lie on either side of the nasal bone. Pressure is exerted on the nose by means of thick reins attached to the back of the noseband. Riding in these bridles requires special knowledge and skills, and they must be fitted correctly to avoid damage or discomfort to the horse.

Some readers may remember Eddy Macken, the Irish international showjumper, jumping one of his horses in a hackamore. Because he was so skilful in riding difficult horses, he could use unconventional devices to get results, but this does not mean that the average rider can do the same. A one-off solution to a particular horse's problem is not a cue for the rest of the riding world to turn it into a fashionable gadget. You must know why you may need an unusual bit for your horse, and also know how to use it without causing your horse pain, because in the long term they make horses pull in their attempt to escape the pain. Severe bits are never the long-term answer, even if they appear to work at first. Your main aim is to obtain the horse's obedience, understanding, balance and fitness, so that it can accept the bit with confidence.

Nosebands

THE DROP NOSEBAND

The drop noseband will affect the action of the bit. It should be used only with a snaffle bit and with a clear understanding of how it fits the horse. The purpose of the drop noseband is to prevent the horse from opening its mouth to evade the bit. If the horse opens its mouth or crosses its jaw, the bit will ride up into the corners of its mouth. This type of noseband must be fitted well above the horse's nostrils, and

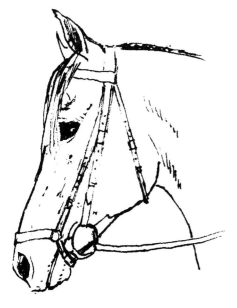

Drop noseband fitted too low.

Drop noseband fitted correctly.

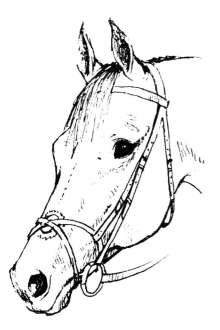

The Grakle noseband.

Flash noseband with Fulmer snaffle.

the strap at the back should lie in the curb groove behind its lower jaw. The strap in the curb groove should not be so tight that it prevents the horse from moving its mouth at all. It must be able to relax its lower jaw and to chew the bit gently.

The fitting of the noseband should be tested by inserting a finger between the strap at the back of the jaw and the sharp jawbone; testing the fitting at the front will not suffice. The drop noseband must be the correct size for each horse. If it is too wide it will not lie on top of the bit, and if too narrow it will pull the cheek-straps too far forward and out of alignment. The front part of the noseband must be firm enough to prevent it from dropping down too near the horse's nostrils, while the strap behind the jaw should be long enough to allow for adjustment to be made according to the horse's reaction to the noseband.

THE GRAKLE

The Grakle or crossed noseband is designed to prevent the horse from crossing its jaw, and from pulling. It has two straps, which cross over each other higher up on the horse's face than the drop noseband. The upper strap goes above the bit, the lower one below the bit, and they are fastened one above the other at the back of the jaw. The upper strap can be fastened slightly tighter than the lower one, but as both of them press on the jawbone they should be fitted without exerting unnecessary pressure.

THE FLASH

The flash noseband has a cavesson noseband, as used with the basic bridle, but it also has a small loop attached to the front of it through which a thinner strap is inserted. The strap is then passed round the back of the horse's jaw in the same way as the drop noseband and fastened on the near side of the horse's head. The flash noseband serves a similar purpose to the drop noseband, although the loop prevents the flash from being fitted too low on the horse's nose.

My advice is to avoid using these gadgets if you can. If the situation does warrant their use then fit them humanely and slacken them off gradually until you no longer need them. Too many riders who use these auxiliary nosebands seem to think they should be tightened up like a girth, and I often have to point out to novice riders the pain they are causing in this way. Often the noseband is done up so tightly that I have to struggle to undo it. To get some idea of the pain of a tight noseband, try pressing hard on your own nose and jawbones for a few minutes and see what it feels like.

Saddles and Saddlery

The earliest saddles were probably made of wood, and are still made of this material in Peru and Mongolia. For those who require a more comfortable medium between themselves and their horses, a modern saddle can be one of the most expensive outlays after the horse. A good leather saddle can cost £450 or more, though using synthetic material can reduce the cost considerably.

Serious thought should be given to the purchase of a saddle. The weight of the saddle should rest on the muscle on either side of the horse's spine. If the saddle does not fit properly it may press or pinch the spine, or the weight of it and the rider will be distributed unevenly, causing uneven pressure on the muscles. A correctly fitted saddle is a must if you wish the horse to be pain-free and minimally encumbered by this unnatural weight on its back. Any anomalies can cause bruising and sores, which sometimes go unobserved for long periods.

I write from long experience, having had to point out to riders of all levels that their horses' backs are often painful. There should be no tenderness when you press on the back muscle. The saddle should clear the spine by the width of two fingers inserted under the pommel when the rider is mounted, leaving a clear space at the back of the saddle. If the padding is flat or the saddle is not balanced, this part too can press on the spine. The centre should be the lowest part when viewed from the side, and when the rider is mounted there should be room for the width of a hand between the seat and the back of the saddle. The saddle should be the right size for the rider as well as the horse.

A saddle needs restuffing about once a year, depending on the amount you use it. I advocate a daily check on mounting, to make sure that any change in the horse's condition and the saddle padding has not combined to bring the saddle dangerously close to the withers. During my freelance years of teaching I was frequently confronted with this problem. I solved it temporarily by rolling up the flaps of the numnah as substitute padding to lift the saddle clear of the horse's spine. The saddle may look somewhat perched up on its back, but once the rider is mounted it settles into place. Some riders seem to think that the numnah as used normally serves the same purpose. In fact it increases the pressure over the withers by filling up the space.

General-purpose saddle.

Dressage saddle.

There are different saddles for different activities, but unless you specialize seriously a good general-purpose saddle should suffice. Before laying out a lot of money for a saddle, sit on your horse bareback to appreciate just which muscles are going to support it, and to some extent be suppressed by the weight of it when it is in place. I think you may be surprised at what you discover. The pain you may experience from sitting on its bare back is nothing to what the horse will suffer from the weight of you and your saddle pressing down on it.

The saddle attachments, such as stirrup leathers, irons and girths should also be chosen carefully. Leathers should be the right length for adjustment; irons should be of a safe width, so that the foot does not slip through (if the iron is too wide) or become stuck (if it is too narrow). I find that synthetic materials are difficult to manipulate, especially nylon stirrup leathers. Girths are available in various designs and materials, so go for pliability, easy cleaning, and ease of adjustment when mounted. Make sure that the girth is long enough to do up easily, but not so long that the buckles end up at the top of the girth straps. The right size will allow for variations in your horse's condition.

You may be interested in the following story about the origin of stirrup treads. It began before the Second World War when I was doing my training with Jane Butt, a friend to whom I owed my

109

examination success. We lost touch during the war, but not long afterward we met again. By this time she had married, and with her husband had designed stirrup treads out of old bicycle tyres. She asked me to try them out. At that time no one showed much interest, but I was full of praise for this invention. No more smooth irons or cold feet in winter! I doubt if Jane ever took out a patent on her ingenious idea, and she certainly never foresaw the future popularity for a device so simple yet such a boon to riders everywhere.

Equestrian equipment for the horse and rider has never been more varied, and new concepts are coming on to the market all the time. One of the most innovative is the adjustable saddle tree, a boon to horse owners if it proves successful. Another breakthrough, which I think benefits the horse, is the design and materials used for horse clothing. These are now lighter and better fitting, and the range is extensive.

I regret that it is difficult to find a saddler who makes saddles to measure, but on the whole the area of saddlery has made much progress in producing safe equipment for present-day requirements. These are often more comfortable for the horse, provided proper attention is paid to fitting, quality and maintenance. If you are not sure about your needs, do not be afraid to ask for advice. It will save money and disappointment in the long term.

8 Problems for Riders

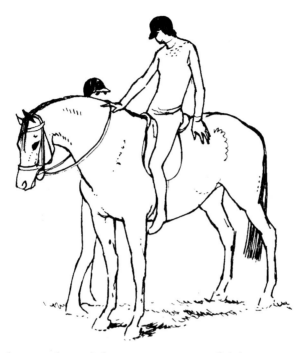

Riders, like their horses, have inherent difficulties to contend with in their training. To begin with there is the question of your bodily proportions: some of us are simply more suited for riding than others. Then there is your temperament, and the way it it might affect your relationship with the horse. To assess your potential as a rider, you must take into account your physical, mental and emotional state. While you can learn a lot from a good teacher, self-knowledge can be just as useful as knowledge provided by an expert.

Blocks to Learning

Many physical problems arise from mental difficulties. Fear accounts for about 85 per cent of tightness or stiffness, and often lies at the root of imbalance and lack of co-ordination. If I list some of the common anxieties from which riders can suffer, you may recognize some of your own:

- Fear of falling off.
- Fear of losing control.
- Fear of hurting yourself.
- Fear of not understanding what the teacher wants.
- Fear of being shouted at.

Teachers need to be more understanding and realize the extent to which these hidden worries affect a pupil's performance, and to remember that pupils become mentally and physically tired much more quickly than we realize. I have learnt from experience how important it is not to have unrealistic expectations of riders. Each rider's goals need to be kept within range of what can be achieved, otherwise they will feel they have failed if they do not reach them. The teacher's goals are sometimes better undisclosed while you help your pupils to reach the targets they set for themselves.

'A trouble shared is a trouble halved' is a very true maxim; it is always worth discussing your anxieties with a friend or teacher. The recognition of fear reduces it at once, and will release some of your physical tension, tension which you may not even have been aware of.

From the rider's point of view we have to examine the attitudes that govern the way we think and feel. The mind–body link is one that any rider can usefully learn to cultivate, especially when working with a living partner of another species. When horse and rider are in full contact with each other, the horse is constantly picking up signals from the rider's body language. How we handle the horse on the ground before we mount, and how we sit on its back, provides the horse with a constant flow of information. This is why it is important for riders to learn how to handle their minds as well as their bodies if they wish to ride a horse with confidence.

A Positive Attitude

Since our mind influences our physical state, it is well worth developing positive thought habits. By nature we often tend to be pessimistic, which can become very self-defeating, but there is no need to become stuck in this mode.

How, for example, do you feel about your body? We only have to read a magazine or watch the television to realize that the body beautiful is the one that receives most publicity. The inevitable result is that most people are dissatisfied with their physical appearance, as is obvious when listening to friends who are dieting or comments made when you are buying clothes. Do you know anyone who has not wished that some part of their anatomy could be changed?

Self-consciousness is at its height when all, or nearly all, is revealed in a swimsuit, or when donning a leotard for keep-fit classes. The same is increasingly true of riding now that stretch material makes breeches cling to the body. Gone are the days of the baggy wings of the old-fashioned non-stretch cavalry twill, which could cover a multitude of sins and keep you warm as well. In winter you can still envelop your upper half in a voluminous anorak, but not in the summer when you want to ride in a shirt.

Today's riding kit follows our contours and can easily make us feel self-conscious, which can lead to anxiety and negativity. If this is a problem you have, try the following exercise. Make a list of all the negative things you say to yourself about your looks, and see whether each one is really true. Then make a list of what you feel good about and are thankful to possess. Good health might be a blessing with which you could start.

Physical Proportions and Balance

Small people may moan about their lack of stature, but they do have advantages when riding. They are able to ride small horses and ponies which are often such

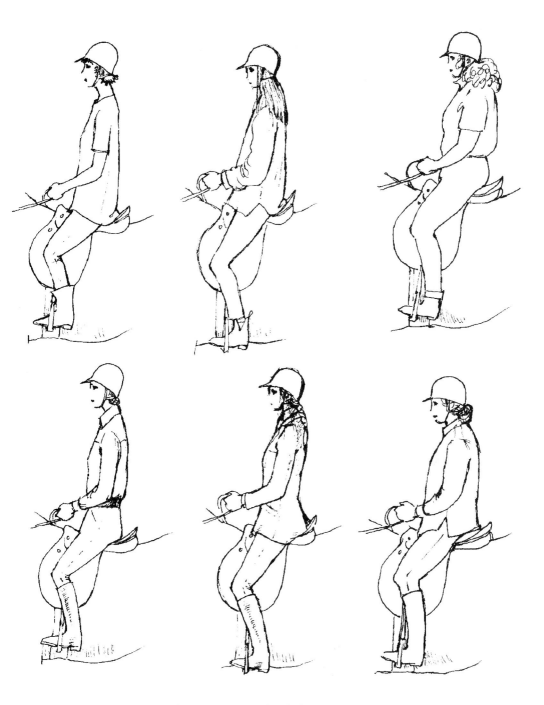

You can make the best of yourself by wearing suitable clothes.

fun; in fact they are in a position to ride almost any size of horse, whereas a tall person tends to be 'under-horsed' if a large animal is not available. If they have sufficient self-confidence there is no reason at all why a small person cannot be a 'big person' inside, and professional riders who are small in stature often create this impression.

Shortness is just one of the common 'problems' in which rider can get bogged down. Other apparent difficulties – and I have seen pupils being nagged at by their teachers because of them – include short arms, a long back, short legs, fat thighs, round shoulders, stiff ankles, a hollow back, and not knowing left from right. This list indicates several areas of the body which can interfere with balance, and the combination of 'problems' can cause instructors to become so impatient that their pupils cannot respond effectively.

This can make a pupil obsessive about a particular difficulty. I had a case recently when a pupil who had been riding with me regularly developed a tightness in her right leg. After she had practised some awareness exercises, the difficulty was found to be in her ankle, a legacy of having been nagged to turn in her toes. She discovered that even when she was at rest there was an unconscious tendency to keep up this tension, even though it was two years since she had ridden in this way. It is as if the muscles have their own memory which keeps carrying out previous orders, even when we think they have been countermanded by our conscious mind. Once this has been discovered the habit will be more easily rectified.

Those of you who have long backs will know that such elegance can have the disadvantage of weakness. A long back gives a lovely silhouette, but needs to be supported by strong muscles, which can be usefully developed through exercises when you are dismounted. If the long-backed person also has short arms, the place where their hands should be carried will be considerably higher than that usually recommended by teachers who insist on the hands being kept down. 'Where is down?' you might well ask. Is it on the neck, on the withers, or just above the withers? The answer is that it is where each individual feels that their hands are not interfering with their balance. When viewed from the side there should be a straight line from the rider's elbow down through the forearm, the hand, the rein and the bit. If the hands are too high, this line will be broken just in the same way that it is disturbed when they are pressed down too far. The only problem is that the rider who has to carry the hands rather higher to create this alignment may feel slightly insecure, because the support of the horse's neck is not so readily available. This is a subconscious reaction, because the horse's neck should not be a means of achieving security.

There is no doubt that if the hands are fairly close to the withers the rider automatically feels greater safety. The level of the rider's elbow varies very little unless the shoulders are raised, whereas the head of the horse can be altered to a far greater extent. It is up to the rider's skill to maintain the line from the bit to their elbow whether the horse raises or lowers its head. A rider who has learned to maintain this line has developed what is called 'a balanced seat', entirely independent of the hands.

It is interesting to notice how the level of a rider's elbow can vary from person to person. This of course depends on different individual proportions, some of us

Shirley, who is 5ft 1in, sitting out of balance on a 14hh. horse.

Improving her posture on a 14hh. pony.

Riding without stirrups lengthens her outline.

having short backs and long arms and others having long backs and short arms. Whichever way we are built it is possible to adapt and find a balanced position on the horse.

It is important to find a comfortable position that feels right for your own body, for only when you have found this will you be able to sit on the horse with the minimum of tension. Tension is often caused by trying too hard, and in the end this only magnifies what you are trying to eradicate. Accepting yourself, and liking what you have, is much more likely to bring you the results you are so keen to achieve.

Remember that whatever your physique is like there are other people with the opposite problems, so no one is better off than anybody else. It is very easy to envy those people who seem to have beautiful

figures ideal for riding, but they too will have had their own problems.

Problems like this can arise even with an experienced rider. I was recently working such a rider on the lunge, asking her to carry a foam ball in each hand as she held the reins. When she had got used to doing this, I asked her to drop the reins when she felt ready, so that she was left holding just the balls in her hands. When she did this she was surprised to find that, until she adjusted her balance, she felt slightly insecure, because she had been supporting herself very slightly on the rein tension. This was very difficult for anyone to see as the difference was very subtle, but it became obvious to the rider when she tried this exercise. Such a small discrepancy is difficult for a rider to detect, but easily recognizable to the horse.

Some elegant-looking riders have

Samantha has a long back and long legs.

problems with a hollow back. This may be caused by conformation, tension, or trying to sit up too straight. A habitual posture will be magnified once we are on the horse, whatever form it may take. Few of us deport ourselves with natural grace, nor do we sit as elegantly as we might, and regimes such as the widely available Alexander Technique can teach us the proper use of the body, which in our civilized conditions we seem to have lost along with other natural endowments. As many riders have discovered, we can all learn to improve this state of affairs, and by doing so will find that the results are better than we ever imagined.

Another cause of grievance for some people is short legs. Long legs can provide more contact with the horse's body and greater security. Long legs fit round the ribcage of the horse more easily, making contact below the maximum width of the body, whereas a rider with short legs may feel that their legs barely reach the widest part of the horse. However, I have seen compact stocky riders sitting very deep in the saddle and riding with great competence. Whatever the rider's shape may be, it is important to keep the mass of weight down in the saddle with the legs acting as stabilizers. On one occasion a stocky candidate for one of the more advanced British Horse Society exams rode every horse with unusual skill, and passed her test with flying colours. This just goes to show that it is possible to perform well with whatever physique you have inherited.

Deportment

We need to differentiate between real physical distortions and what we do to our bodies by the way we think about them.

Susan's arms are short and her hands are too low.

Her arms are more relaxed and the rein line is correct.

118

Round shoulders, for example, can develop for psychological reasons as well as physical ones. Sitting at a school desk may well be the start of our slouching habits. Teenagers who shoot up suddenly and outstrip their contemporaries may feel conspicuous, and try to shrink into themselves. Girls are particularly prone to this defensive posture as they mature. Sometimes people become locked up in their shoulders, and it is difficult for them to recover their normal poise. Much depends on whether there is skeletal change under the muscular tension.

Jane had many years of experience as a rider and horse owner, but was not exempt from postural problems in her overall performance. For a few years there was a lapse in our contact with one another, and when we met again I realized that she had not progressed at all and no one had been able to help her. So I suggested a

Janet has high-set elbows and carries her hands higher to compensate.

Janet, who is 5ft 2in, sitting comfortably on a 15hh. Welsh Cob.

119

Janet trying too hard. Her back and arms are stiff and her legs are contracted.

Letting go.

Janet's improved deportment has resulted in horse and rider moving in balance.

Janet on a 17hh. horse. Here, her good deportment has compensated for her height.

This shows where each rider's legs are placed on the ribcage of their horses.

more relaxed approach, in which she should start to feel comfortable instead of correct. I told her that I was not going to instruct her, but rather direct her attention to what was needed.

I left her for a few moments to settle down, and then asked her to concentrate on comfort. I gave her the freedom to sit any way she liked, and begin to feel her body becoming more at ease. As I watched I was surprised to see that her shoulders had already changed, and it became clear that this was where her major difficulty lay. After half an hour Jane had decided to lengthen her stirrups two holes, which helped to lengthen her back. She was amazed at the way she felt, and at how much better her horse was behaving.

This simple exercise in awareness and relaxation had unlocked all the problems that Jane had been holding in her body for

years. She had been trying too hard, as a result becoming shorter and shorter in her back and her legs. This transformation from a small crouched person to an elegant rider was proof of the adverse power that anxiety and excessive effort can have over our bodies.

It is easier said than done to see ourselves as others see us. One useful technique, once we become immune to the shock of seeing ourselves on screen, is to watch ourselves on video. Even hearing our own voice on a tape recorder can help us to become more self-aware. It takes time to use these gadgets without being self-conscious, but they can be an excellent way of getting to know ourselves, and through them we can explore our reactions in particular situations. They make it possible to see where self-consciousness shows in your body, and what it does to

Susan, who is 5ft 7in, has short legs and needs to work without stirrups.

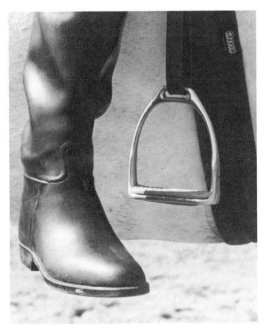

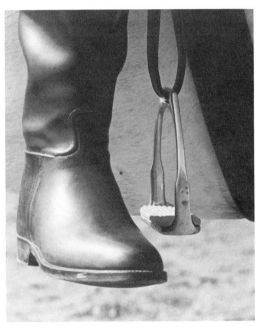

Length of stirrup leather before relaxation.

Stirrup leather adjusted after working without stirrups.

Janet showing the effect of tension on herself and on her horse.

Rounding the back also affects the horse.

The horse responding to her improved deportment.

your voice. It took me a lifetime to recognize the tension in my facial muscles, and it was only by seeing and hearing myself that I learned to take control of my face instead of allowing it to control me.

In Chapter 9 there is an overall body relaxation sequence, which may be helpful in transforming your self-consciousness into 'self-knowing consciousness'. It is not constructive to denigrate ourselves, for everyone is unique. If you were different, however much you might wish to be, you would not be the person that your loved ones accept.

It is not fair to the horse to expect it to perform athletically and obediently if we are unaware of our own body and movement. Actions are clues to the way we think, and it is so true that they speak louder than words. The main quality to develop is that of confident intention, because we move according to how we think.

Learning Guidelines

Here are some routines which can help to unwind an over-tense body and a too-busy mind:

- Keep your attention on one thing at a time.
- Do not expect your horse to cope with more than one point of attention at a time.
- Make sure your goals are realistic and well defined.
- Check your own balance and signals before blaming the horse.
- Listen to your horse as well as expecting it to listen to you.
- Be aware of the horse's fatigue, boredom, pain and confusion.
- Trust your intuition.
- Try to maintain a positive attitude and avoid being judgemental.

125

Both you and your horse have shorter periods of concentration than you might think. An adult's attention span is about ten minutes and a child's is five; your horse's is probably even less. Trying too hard only makes you and the horse tense and stiff. The more aware you are, the more interested you will become in what is happening in the present moment. It is only then that relaxation will take place, much to the relief of your horse.

Your horse will prove to be an infallible reference point as it responds to your physical and mental adjustments. As my own visual awareness has improved, I often see these small shifts of emphasis between the horse and rider as they work on a project together. Sometimes, when I am about to direct a rider, that rider will make the move anyway, even before I have spoken.

We must not forget that the horse has a wonderful ability to tolerate and adapt to human idiosyncrasies, provided certain qualities in the rider are present. If horses did not have this in-built flexibility, they would not perform as well as they do in difficult circumstances. The main ingredient in a happy but unorthodox partnership where finesse and balance seem to be lacking is probably the rider's love of the horse and the natural ability to relax and blend with it.

Nerves

When you have experienced the harmony that it is possible for you and your horse to enjoy, your ambitions may rise, and you might feel that you need the stimulus of competition. Some of us are naturally very competitive, while for others a competition is just a day out to enjoy. The stress that arises when you appear in public can produce a regression to old defensive habits, and so affect the performance for which you spent so much time practising. A common comment after a disappointing competition is, 'But my horse goes so well at home.' Of course it does, because there are no distractions and you are more relaxed. The stress is increased when you ride in front of the judge in a new environment. Doing well and winning are the only goals you have in your mind, even though you know that trying too hard adds to the tension building up inside you.

If competing is for you, it can be illuminating to look more closely at what winning means on a personal level. The most natural reaction to the word 'winning' is its association with success. It implies that when you win you have succeeded. What does 'success' mean to you?

I, like most people, have been conditioned throughout my life to think that winning and achieving our goals can guarantee fulfilment. Most of us think of losing and failing as negative, largely because we forget how much learning we can gain from the experience of 'losing'. Winning makes us feel better than our opponents; it boosts our morale and indicates how our standards compare with our rivals. In competitions, the will to win is half the battle, but it can produce desperation instead of success. If it makes us try so hard that we become tense in our performance, it will detract from it. If we let our minds become distracted and anxious, a small error can turn into a catastrophe. This often arises because our attention becomes spread over too many areas of performance. We are more likely to succeed if we can keep things in perspective, refusing to let the odd lapse interfere with our focused attention on one particular aspect of the game. I find it difficult to do this. I tend to focus on too many things at once, so it has been a useful exercise for me to learn to become more attentive to one activity at a time.

I have found it very useful to look at why winning is so important to me. I was always much more competitive than I ever admitted. 'I am not really competitive,' I have said to myself on numerous occasions, but I now recognize that this was not the whole truth by any means. The fact is that unless I was winning, or my pupils were, I felt a certain insecurity. I did not even enjoy winning with a second-rate performance that I felt was undeserving of a win. Now I view competition from a slightly different angle.

This brings me to the process of reaching winning form, which is really the most important part of the experience of competition. Goal-setting means being quite clear about what you want. When I was younger I had not learned about goal-setting, and my mind was totally goal-orientated. I did not know how to define my goal and then forget about it, giving my full attention to the process of getting there. The way to do this is explained in my book *Natural Riding*, and many other useful books on this subject are now available. The art is to learn to trust the technique that you choose to use, and your success depends on the skill with which you define your goal.

I have found some of my successes to be beneficial because they bring positive feedback on my efforts and improve my life in some way, but others have been short-lived. Fame can take its toll, and many names that hit the headlines are soon forgotten. While you may yearn for the happiness that success is supposed to bring, there are plenty of examples where just the opposite is the result.

It is useful to remember that your winning means that someone else is losing; maybe a lot of other people. You cannot play a sport without there being a losing side or opponent. Your triumph depends on their defeat; they are part of your victory. Have you ever thought of it like that? Have you imagined what it must be like to be a losing rider or a losing horse as a result of your winning? The usual handshaking after a competition acknowledges that some of the competitors have beaten some of the others. Do you ever wonder what is going on in the winners' minds? Do the winners really appreciate their opposition, or do they gloat over them? What do the losers feel about their defeat?

There is a hidden opponent which can be more formidable than any other, and that is yourself. This competition with your own standards, your personal best, can be a real driving force, and is often operating when we don't enjoy the victories we feel we deserve. If this inner voice becomes a critical judge, it can defeat you before you begin. You must learn to feed yourself positive thoughts as you prepare for a challenge. If winning is a crutch to your self-esteem and you feel good only because you are better than someone else, you need to investigate your motivation. If we can explore our motives in wanting to win, we can achieve fulfilling success while enjoying the process instead of being a slave to it, and so avoid exploiting the horse in our drive to succeed.

Being Realistic

Perfectionists – those who set such high standards for themselves and others that

127

the goals are often out of reach – are bound to experience a sense of failure. We all make this error from time to time, and so become disappointed with ourselves. To expect perfection is to court defeat, and the strain of living up to unrealistic standards is bound to detract from happiness and health. If you are a rider it will give your horse one hell of a life. High standards of performance are reached through developing your talents in a balanced, disciplined and realistic way.

I once watched an experienced rider training her dressage horse. During an interval I asked her what she thought she was achieving. She replied with a long list of what was going wrong, so I asked her to look for some positive things, some bright spots. Then I invited her to choose what she felt was the most difficult aspect of her problems, the one that she would most like to overcome. I asked her to concentrate on it without being critical. This approach ironed out the difficulty in a very short time, and also most of the others about which she had complained. We then discussed how she had been feeling initially: 'Oh,' she said, 'I was saying to myself that I would never be ready for the competition at the weekend.'

Not surprisingly this had set a negative and critical tone to her whole practice session. After she had thought about this for a few moments, she came back to me and said, 'Of course, my horse was telling me that I had set an unrealistic goal because I was anxious.'

It always helps to set goals that you have a reasonable chance of achieving. As well as having the 'big goal', try setting smaller goals, one for each lesson. If you do this in a systematic way, there is nothing to stop you having a 'miracle goal' on your horizon.

The subconscious mind has an amazing capacity to deliver the results if we can supply its computer-like workings with appropriate information. Like the computer, however, it is only as good as the information that is fed into it. We need to provide it with a whole range of sensory observation and information, allowing our imagination and intuition as much scope as our intellects. This can be achieved by using the whole range of our sensory skills: sight, sound, smell, hearing, feeling, even our sixth sense which provides flashes of inspiration out of the blue.

Our contact with the animal world makes us realize how insensitive we have become. The horse's ability to comprehend and adapt to our demands is quite remarkable. To see an advanced dressage horse performing is a humbling experience. I am often left wondering how things would turn out if we reversed roles, and how we would cope if we suddenly found ourselves in the horse's place. If there were a magic wand which could be waved to give us this experience, how much better we would understand our horses and the problems with which we present them when we ride.

9 Harnessing your Inner Resources

It is my aim in this chapter to draw your attention to your overall level of fitness, and to suggest ways of improving it without necessarily getting on to the horse. It seems rather unfair to climb on a horse without any preparation, and expect it to become supple instantaneously when we are often as stiff as boards. The horse should not be used like a piece of apparatus in the gymnasium – but it often is.

I always give my pupils time to limber up before they mount, and ask them to do a few deep breathing exercises to help them relax. We then spend a few minutes communicating with the horse, taking time to acknowledge and connect with one another. This preparation makes all the difference to the horse and rider's attitude to each other. This is particularly so in a riding school where horses experience rapid changes of riders, and can easily become impersonal and disinterested.

I am not averse to a titbit being given as an occasional reward, but if it is to be seen as a reward it is best offered at the end of the lesson, and should not be given if the horse is being rude and demanding. Some horses can become very bossy; if this happens it is advisable to stop the reward.

Dismounted Training

For those of you who are short of time and funds, a training regime can be accelerated to some extent without the horse needing to be present. This has been very obvious on 'Natural Riding' courses I have organized, where the dismounted seminars did a great deal to help people to understand what was happening to them in the lessons. During these sessions they had time to mull over events without the distraction of the horse.

In ideal circumstances, and when time and space permit, I encourage my pupils to practise what I call awareness exercises, which involve both mind and body. Feeling the difference between relaxation and tension, for example, can give a rider a much better sense of control. Later in this chapter I shall outline a simple relaxation exercise that anyone can try.

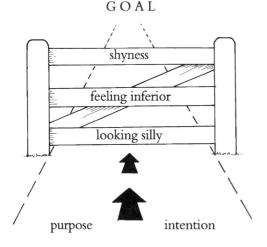

What is getting in the way of your path towards your goal?

Especially in the early stages of learning to ride there can be a sense of 'wasting time' between rides. If you are not careful this can result in feeling pressurized when you ride again, because you feel impelled to make the most of it and to expect too much from yourself and the horse. This is another reason why dismounted exercises can be so helpful.

New Habits for Old

I suggest you begin your self-awareness programme by deciding how much time you can realistically give to it. This will give you some idea about what you think is realistic, and help you to recognize that you have already become involved in goal-setting.

Next, ask yourself what you want to achieve or enjoy in your riding, and what is getting in the way. Is it emotional or physical? If it is emotional, notice how your feelings and thoughts affect your body, for they inevitably will. If on the other hand you think your goals are primarily physical, it is worth checking how these physical goals are related to your thoughts. Is stiffness simply a physical discomfort, for example, or is it also an imbalance related to your mental attitude? What is going on in your head when you feel physically insecure? If you have an old injury, for instance, there can still be subconscious protection taking place, evidence of which I described in my book *Natural Riding* (*see* Further Reading).

Asking yourself questions such as these helps you to become more aware of yourself in many ways: Where do you want to go? Why do you want to achieve it? When do you want to reach it? What are the options available? How committed are you? Once you have clear answers to questions such as these, you are much more likely to succeed with the actual training process.

I always advocate simplicity and brevity rather than complexity, for the simple reason that there is then more chance of keeping up a regime of self-awareness exercises. I think ten minutes is long enough to start with. This is a few minutes longer than a novice dressage test, and will help you empathize with the way you expect your horse to pay attention for a similar time-span. Ten minutes can seem a very long time, and to the horse it must seem even longer.

WORKING IN PAIRS AND GROUPS

Working with other riders can also be very revealing, because it helps to simulate the partnership between horse and rider.

With my pupils I sometimes use what I call the 'hand to hand' exercise. Dismounted, they work in pairs with their open hands held up in front of them, with a small space in between the two people. I ask them to make contact with one another's hands as slowly as they possibly can. When they have done this, one person in each pair moves their hands in circles while the other person follows their movements, still keeping the same light contact. They then change roles.

When I first did this exercise myself I discovered that my partner was very dominating when she had the active role, and was very rigid in the passive one. This made me aware of both the timidity and the aggression of which my partner was capable. If I had been a horse and she the rider, these qualities would have been even more immediately apparent. The new insights that came from this exercise led to a considerable improvement in the way in which all the riders used their reins.

As many pair exercises involve physical contact, changing partners can help to demonstrate how different we all are in the degrees of resistance we experience with different human and equine partners. When pupils explore their partner's reactions, they can often relate this experience to their contact with different horses. On one occasion I noticed that some of my pupils were very self-conscious about their physical contact with each other. I told them to shut their eyes and imagine that they were all horses, making physical contact with other horses. This soon broke the ice. There is no doubt that working with a group of riders in this way can bring about some amazing results. It seems as if the pooling of experience proves the saying that the sum of the parts is greater than the whole.

My first experience of this factor occurred during one of my Natural Riding courses. It was so well attended that I had to divide the class into two groups. One group was made up of very novice riders, and the other included riders of more varied experience. Both classes came together for the dismounted sessions, and this was followed by one group riding while the other watched them. Then they changed over. The discussions that followed the riding and observation activities accelerated everyone's awareness enormously. Every one of the pupils, both novice and more advanced, gained insights into their own problems and attitudes through sharing their own experiences with others.

For the last session they all rode together in a large arena, where each rider

131

worked on a theme they had chosen. The harmony and control was quite amazing, and the overall improvement was unbelievable. I think that the whole group had been empowered and integrated through their shared awareness.

WILLPOWER

However we work with our self-awareness, self-discipline is the key to success. The numerous examples of sportsmen and women who have successfully used

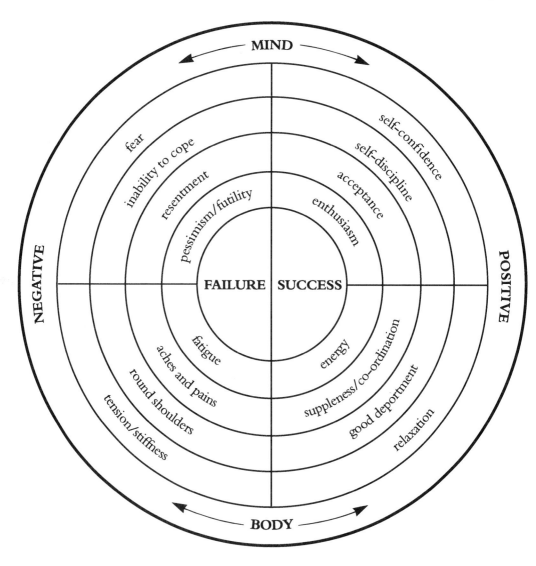

The physical and mental manifestations of positive and negative attitude, and the way in which attitudes of the mind and body interact with each other.

mental rehearsal techniques prove that we can progress even while sitting on our own in a chair. This realization will, I hope, encourage you to keep going with whatever technique suits you best.

It is very easy to become sidetracked and forget about self-discipline. I readily admit to being easily diverted and having difficulty in picking up from where I left off. This tends to make me rush through commitments in the hope that I can complete them before there is another distraction, or before I run out of steam. I am still working on this, but I do know that dismounted exercises work for me.

If you can summon up the willpower to make one small step a day, you will undoubtedly reap unexpected rewards. You may not recognize these rewards at first because the changes are so subtle, but before long they will become more obvious, and the feedback from your efforts will start to bring encouragement, interest, awareness, relaxation and true conviction.

RELAXATION

Conscious relaxation is one of my favourite self-awareness techniques. Here is a simple relaxation exercise that you can practise whenever you feel the need to stop and recover your inner balance. Find yourself a space to lie on the floor on something soft, a rug or a folded-up blanket. Put a book on the floor beside you (I will explain why in a minute), and cover yourself with a light blanket. The use of soothing music can help you to relax and breathe properly.

With your legs straight and your arms by your sides, start by stretching your left leg downwards as far as it will go. Pointing your toes, hold this tension until the muscles begin to tremble, then relax. Do the same with the right leg, then with both legs, then relax. Now put the book on your tummy and take three deep breaths. Watch to see how far the book rises and falls as you inhale and exhale.

It is important to fill the lower part of your lungs rather than simply lifting your chest and shoulders. If the book is rising and falling only a short distance, try breathing further down into the bottom of your lungs, and see what this feels like. Now relax for a few seconds before doing a similar exercise for your arms.

Having removed the book, push your left arm down towards your feet, with your fingers spread out as far as they will go. Keep pushing down until the muscles begin to tremble, and then relax. Repeat this with your right arm, and then with

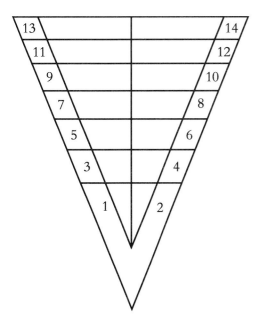

Shade in the days when you practise relaxation exercises. A pattern to indicate the extent of your self-discipline will emerge.

133

both arms together. Now replace the book on your tummy and take three more deep breaths. See if you notice any difference about the way you are breathing.

Replace the book on the floor before doing the final stretch. This involves pushing both legs and arms out as far as possible. Hold this full-body stretch and keep breathing until you feel the muscles beginning to tremble as they tire. Now relax and take three more deep breaths. If you have the time and the energy you can repeat the whole process once more. Otherwise, lie still for a few moments savouring the sense of relaxation, until you feel at peace.

The beauty of this exercise is that it is easy to do, does not take long, and emphasizes the difference between tension and relaxation. This helps to make us more aware of the residual tension we have acquired over the years. Never push yourself too hard; always work within a comfortable range of physical effort, and do your exercises slowly. It is surprisingly taxing to move in this controlled way, though you will be rewarded with a pleasant sense of mild fatigue. When you have done this relaxation exercise, it will be interesting to see whether you can breathe in this way when you are standing up or sitting in the saddle.

Always try to avoid any temptation to force your breath. Allow a pause just before you inhale, and let the breath move in to fill your lungs. The chances are that you will soon be breathing more deeply without thinking about it. Breath is life; even if you have no time to spare for anything else, do learn how to breathe efficiently so that your body and mind benefit. Too many people spend their lives running on half rations of oxygen. This deprivation can be rectified so easily

if we take just a few moments each day to practise how to draw breath most effectively.

Having talked about the benefits of breathing exercises for the rider, we might usefully turn our attention to the horse. Until we humans started to put the horse under unnatural amounts of stress, it too maintained a natural and rhythmical way of breathing. It took me a considerable length of time to realize just how much a horse will change its pattern of breathing when it is tense. Once you become breath-conscious, you will start to notice the breathing patterns of different horses in different situations. I always used to connect rapid breathing with overwork and unfitness, without taking the stress factor into consideration. Now that I am more aware of what stresses both humans and horses feel, I am sure that domesticated horses hold their breath when they are anxious just as we do. Resistance in the ridden horse is accompanied by an alteration in its breathing.

As my own awareness has developed, I often notice that, when a pupil comes to rest her horse in front of me, the horse will take a deep breath and give a sigh before it relaxes its head and neck. Blowing the nose is another sign that a horse is starting to settle into its work. As we cannot tense up without altering our breathing, neither can the horse, and riders should check both their own respiration and that of the horse. It is a good indication of how relaxed you both are.

A more obvious sign that the horse is holding its breath is when it does so deliberately when the girth is being tightened. This is a defensive reaction on the horse's part to protect itself from this restriction. When it lets its breath go, the girth slackens. This is why riders must check the

134

girth after mounting, and again after a preliminary warm-up. The girth may need to be taken up two or three holes.

Another awareness exercise for the rider is to watch how the horse's belly changes shape, and how the expression on its face changes. It may turn round and try to bite, its tail may swish, and it may stamp its feet or kick to express its disapproval.

The solution is to do up the girth gradually. Try to make adjustments that the horse can tolerate. Allow the horse a few minutes to relax before you take it out to ride. If you want to test what the horse feels, ask a friend to put a tight belt round your own ribcage, which is the part of your anatomy equivalent to where the girth is placed on the horse.

AFFIRMATIONS

We now come to the subject of affirmations, positive statements which we can use as a means of counteracting our negative conditioning. You only have to listen to people discussing current affairs or the goings-on of the people they know to recognize how often we fall into negativity. All too often we dwell on the worst aspects of a situation, and our friends are only too happy to support us in our negativity! As a result we can easily feel very critical of ourselves, forgetting all our achievements and good qualities. Every time it happens we reinforce our gloomy self-defeating attitude, a way of looking at ourselves which probably started in childhood.

This is, however, a habit that we can reverse at any age. One practical exercise is to see if you can keep a note of all your negative thoughts for half an hour, and then think what it would cost if you were to put two pence in a charity box for each

one of them. It might surprise you to see how much it amounts to. Think what a difference it would make if you could turn some of those negative thoughts into positive ones instead. There is an opposite side to every coin, but sometimes we never think to turn it over.

I sometimes wonder if the false modesty with which we may have been imbued as a form of good manners is one of the reasons why we find it so hard to recognize our good points and to admit success. I don't know about you, but I can often hear the hidden parent within myself telling me not to boast because it is bad manners. This negative conditioning during our most formative years can still influence our lives years later. Fortunately, though we may have lived with this self-limiting modesty for many years, it can be reversed in a relatively short space of time, so the sooner you get down to some regular affirmations the sooner this magic will work for you. The hardest part is not the time or the effort, but the inserting of a new pattern of thinking amongst your ingrained ones. It is as if there is a deep resistance to any change, but if you persevere you will achieve your just reward.

If this concept is new to you, begin with a very simple affirmation. One that has helped me to establish the habit is saying, 'This is a good morning', whether I feel it is or not. As you persist with this routine, the positive feedback soon becomes obvious, and will provide the impetus to take affirmations into other areas of your life. Where riding is concerned, negative thinking is related to losing control, looking stupid, not being able to canter, being shouted at, or an overwhelming sense of failure. A friend of mine recently came out of a lesson that I had been watching saying, 'Oh my goodness, that was awful. I feel quite hopeless.' No one had said this to her, but her negative thoughts produced such a sense of failure that it clouded the whole experience for her. I suggest that you might use the following affirmations, and others like them, to re-place such self-limiting thoughts:

- When I want to, I can.
- I can jump with confidence.
- I am not afraid of cantering.

Repeat these phrases out loud, even if you feel afraid. Fear in its various guises lies behind most of our hang-ups. The sooner it can be confronted, the sooner it will go away. This will happen when your brain begins to believe the new messages as it erases the old ones.

Always make your affirmations in the present tense, regardless of whether it is happening or not. Keep on saying them night and morning, and during the day whenever there is a moment to spare. This technique can help improve both your riding and the other goals in your life. They help us to replace restricting habits with positive purpose.

THE USE OF IMAGERY

Visualization is another creative way of improving performance without actually being with the horse, and has been proved to be so effective that it is universally practised by top performers in any sport. Visualization involves conscious goal-setting and specific imagination. Like anything else, the more you do it the easier it becomes, and the more you will get out of it.

Before you begin any visualization exer-cises, make sure that you have plenty of time. Find a quiet place, and either lie down on the floor with a pillow and a blanket or sit comfortably in a chair where you can relax. Begin by becoming aware of your breathing, and as you exhale let the tension flow out from your body: your head, face, neck, shoulders, arms, hands, lungs, chest, diaphragm, abdomen and buttock muscles, thighs, calves, ankles and toes.

Be aware of your body becoming heavy and relaxed. When you feel you have let go of your tensions, begin to compose the picture of yourself as you are going to be. Take your time to imagine all the details of how you will look, what you will feel like. When you have used your imaginary senses of touch, temperature, colour, smell and sound, and have absorbed the picture being painted in your mind, let it drift into your memory. Stay quietly wherever you are for a few minutes and take three or four deep breaths as you return to reality.

Now make an affirmation of your choice, such as 'I am close to my horse in the saddle', or 'I enjoy being part of the horse's back when it canters', or 'I can canter smoothly and feel secure', or 'I can sit comfortably with the movement of the canter'. Another useful visualization is to imagine you are the rider you most ad-mire, and to visualize yourself riding as they do.

Once you start to understand the power of affirmations you will find it easier to make up your own. If you do this sort of vizualisation/affirmation exercise often enough, you will find that these images become filed away in the depths of your subconscious mind. You will also find that, alongside the subtle psychological changes, minute physical changes will also be taking place.

Let me give you an example of how

visualization works. If I was wanting to ride a better dressage test than I have ever done, I would picture the place, the exact setting around the arena, and the weather. I would see myself and my horse turned out immaculately, each sequence of movements being performed without any of the habitual problems. I would try to sense the feeling of flowing and floating together through the test, deliberately concentrating on each move from moment to moment. I would do this rehearsal as often as I could, and if I could find a friend who would help by asking me to describe verbally what I was seeing, this would help to enforce the pictures being fed into my subconscious mind.

The Brain

Having explained the techniques of visualization and affirmation, a few words about what happens in your brain as a result of using these techniques may help to strengthen your commitment to them. Although it is simplifying things a little, it is now widely believed that the left and right hemispheres of the brain have fairly well-defined roles in human ability and behaviour.

The left side of our brain is thought to be used more for analytical and academic activities, while the right side is where the artistic abilities, imagery and intuition are primarily located and processed, and where subconscious experience is stored away. Our education is for the most part geared to utilize our left hemisphere, by studying subjects like maths and science and languages. Important though these are, there is a danger that our minds can become filled with facts to the detriment of our more abstract creative qualities.

While we may have a good idea of what we know with our reasoning minds, very few of us know what potential exists to be tapped in the depths of our creative, intuitive minds. This does not mean that we cannot sometimes gain access to this knowledge without being aware of doing so. We often tap this source when we are on a peak of personal performance, when we are playing, dancing or riding superbly and without effort. At times like this we are using the right side of our brain, the source of our inspiration.

A sceptical friend recently borrowed a book from me that teaches you how to draw with the right side of your brain. After she had practised some of the rather unusual exercises suggested in the book she was astounded at the results they produced. Even though she had drawn them upside down, her drawings were vibrant and flowing. Reluctantly she admitted to being aware of having switched from her usual 'left brain' precision into a totally different mode. She found that when she was released from trying too hard she could draw creatively and intuitively.

The mind is most receptive when we are relaxed. It is in this state of relaxation that the power of positive words can seep into our subconscious mind. If we respect and welcome them, they will quickly begin to replace old negative thought patterns and offer us a new lease of life.

Becoming the Other

In the last chapter I suggested that we could become more perceptive about our riding if we were able to use our imagination to 'become' the horse instead of always being the rider. This exercise in role-changing is used in a form of personal therapy called Gestalt. For many people it has been a useful way of helping them to know themselves better. The first time I was involved in this exercise I was pretty sceptical about it. It arose because I was discussing a pupil's persistent riding problems with a friend; my friend suggested trying this technique, and as he did not ride I had to brief him on the facts of the problem.

The pupil concerned was afraid of cantering, a common problem with novices, but one that can sometimes persist indefinitely. My friend asked me to imagine being the pupil who had the problem, and after I had spent a few moments putting myself in that role he asked me how I felt before cantering, at the moment when I asked the horse to canter, and at the moment when the horse responded. I was amazed at finding myself having moments of unexpected insight into another person's experiences. I felt as if I was the pupil, and I began to see her problem much more clearly. As a result, when she had her next lesson we were able to resolve the difficulty. The solution seemed to come from an intuitive source rather than an intellectual one.

I have found this technique for problem solving most useful, even when I am on my own. I find that it helps to use two chairs, moving from one to the other as I change roles. I find that it is important to say who I am by using the name of my new role each time I change chairs. When I 'become' the other person, or the horse for that matter, I give myself a few minutes to imagine myself taking on their personality and appearance.

Though it may sound a little odd, it can help enormously to put your body in different positions in order to 'become' horse and rider. If you use this process to put yourself in the horse's place, try getting down on your hands and knees to simulate its horizontal equilibrium; when you become the rider again, stand up in order to help you sense your vertical stance in relation to the horse. When the natural talents of both your horse and yourself are free to express themselves, you become extensions of each other. It really is time that we dropped false modesty and recognized our real potential, so that this potential can be used to the full. To discover our own full potential as well as that of our horse is to give life another dimension.

Mental Rehearsal

I have found that most horse-lovers tend to have an artistic talent, however dormant it may have become. As children they often used their imagination in playing horses or drawing them. Art and riding seem to appear in tandem, so when it comes to abstract thought and imagery you may be able to rediscover the child within to help you recapture the fantasies that your brain so readily produced when you were young.

When rekindled, this faculty can be put to practical use in visualizing ways of improving your riding; indeed, it can be used to improve your artistic capabilities or any other talents that you may possess. With practice, building mental pictures becomes easier and more precise. This precision is very important, for it is the detail that you can paint into your abstract scene that enforces it on the subconscious.

If, for example, your goal is to be able to canter sitting deeply in the saddle with security and comfort, you might find it useful to imagine the following:

- The horse, its colour and size; imagine feeling close to the horse.
- The place you are in; the scenery around you; birds calling; the smell of hay.
- The weather; the wind blowing in your face.
- Your clothes, and how your body feels.
- What the trot feels like before you canter; when you will ask for the canter; how the transition into canter feels.
- The pounding of the horse's hooves; the rhythm they produce; blending with the flow.

As you imagine these things, let appropriate words come into your mind – feeling free, going with the horse, being the horse, floating, rocking, letting it happen – whatever word or words you find most evocative. Once you have discovered the words that best match your most positive experiences of imaginary riding, you can then use these words to help you when you are on your horse. You will almost certainly find that they help you when you are practising, and in times of stress such as when you are competing.

10 Out and About

In our crowded countryside, humans and horses share ever-decreasing tracts of open space. We all react differently to the place in which we live. Even though sufficient space is not always available, having some territory we can call our own is an important facet of our life. Horses, too, have their ways of reacting to confined areas, and like humans resent any intrusion of their personal space. Just as people who lead reclusive lives can sometimes show signs of eccentricity, horses who are unnaturally confined for long periods will react in a confused way when released. Most horses, like the majority of humans, rejoice in open spaces.

Anyone who intends to keep a horse will be faced with important and some-times difficult decisions about stabling, grazing, and finding somewhere suitable to ride. Adequate space is essential to the health and happiness of the domesticated horse, be it kept indoors or outside, and is relevant to its safety as well as its comfort. Exercising the horse may pose a problem in some areas, as green belts diminish and road traffic increases.

This is one reason for an upsurge of interest in schooling horses, which takes less space but raises further questions about the use of paddocks for grazing. The minimum area for working a horse is about 22 × 44yd (20 × 40m).

A neighbour of mine recently came up against the perennial problem of finding enough space for her two horses. Until recently she had unrestricted use of the forest on our doorstep. She also has the use of three fields for grazing, and considers herself lucky to have these facilities. Times change, however, and so do forestry rules and the encroachment of building projects. The first limits the use of the forest tracks, the second her grazing, which seriously affects her winter feeding programme.

Another problem arises as she has recently developed an interest in dressage. She cannot practise at home because there are no flat areas in her field, so unless she transports her horses to the nearest indoor school she cannot practise her dressage. Here she is in a cleft stick because she does not own a trailer.

The influence of space on particular animals is well illustrated by this situation: her old horse enjoys its forest excursions, but her younger mare has never become accustomed to the dappled light, which causes it to shy violently. Yet this mare will work with enthusiasm in the security of the indoor school. Her two horses demonstrate opposite reactions to their different environments.

This situation, where riders are confined to restricted riding areas and cannot join in local club activities unless they can cadge a lift or have their own means of getting there, is not uncommon. The difficulties faced by riders today are finding adequate nearby space for their equestrian needs, and having access to transport if a wider range of enjoyment is to be experienced. Transit vehicles present another responsibility for horse owners and, like horses, need maintaining and handling.

It may seem that farmers' families must

Traffic hazards.

141

have the ideal setting for riding on their doorstep, but this is not always true. Farmers are often too conscientious to permit indiscriminate use of precious land, and can be very grudging about keeping a horse when it is such a wasteful grazer.

Golden beaches can lure the rider, too, but they may not be as ideal as they appear. There may be council restrictions on riding, quicksands which can be a nightmare, and dangerous tides which pose a threat to the unwary. I am highlighting these various points to temper the enthusiasm of would-be horse owners. The confines that restrict today's rider are a million years away from the open spaces experienced by the natural horse.

In view of these limitations on both horses and riders it is not surprising that equestrian competitions have become so well supported. They provide the opportunities to meet other riders, ride cross-country, and to take part in dressage and showjumping. With the indoor facilities that are now available, some of these events can still continue in winter. This interest in riding has encouraged more riders to seek instruction to improve their performance, and as a result standards continue to improve. This naturally leads to pupils wanting practice facilities at home, such as a jumping paddock or an outdoor arena where training can continue on a regular basis. This brings us back to the question of how this room is to be found. Incentive, insight and ingenuity can often find a way.

Your own Manège

If, after due consideration, having your own arena becomes a priority, I suggest careful planning and the advice of someone who has had the experience of

Susan's manège.

142

constructing one. The specific location will often dictate to a large extent what is possible, and what works in one place may not be feasible in another. The quality of certain types of material, for example, may stand up more satisfactorily to your local weather conditions. There are firms who specialize in all-weather surfaces, but not all of them are infallible, and they can be expensive.

A good schooling area needs regular maintenance: the track must be raked daily and the surface harrowed at intervals to keep it level and loose; it must be sprayed in dry weather, and the surface topped up from time to time. The more it is used, the more attention it will require. The same considerations apply to indoor arenas. From what my pupils tell me, once they have been initiated into the benefits of riding a well-trained horse most of them would like regular access to a good schooling area. It will always enhance the rewards of riding a well-balanced and supple horse. The danger is that this is just the thin end of the financial wedge as riders want to become more experienced!

One of the dangers of schooling is that the rider can become too absorbed in the process of schooling to the detriment of other activities. Another problem arises with horses who are said to be traffic-proof or, more dramatically, 'bomb-proof'. Horses can become disorientated if they are restricted to an indoor riding school for too long. From experience I have found that my bomb-proof horses are no longer reliable in traffic after a spell in the school. This suggests that horses must be kept in contact with traffic if they are to keep up their tolerance of it. Road work and cross-country expeditions should be part of any horse's regular routine.

Riding in Company

It is difficult to assess the proportion of riders who ride in company, compared with those who most often ride on their own. The horse, being a social animal, enjoys going out with its friends and, if this is not a usual occurrence, its *savoir-faire* may well evaporate. The distraction of other horses can be too much for the horse who is usually isolated, in which case its manners can go overboard.

Getting cross with an animal in this hot-headed mood will not help, and the wise course is to keep as calm as possible until you can remove it from the situation. This may be easier said than done, depending on how considerate your riding companions happen to be. If they ride on regardless of your plight, you may well find your horse becoming uncontrollable.

One of the disciplines in my riding school was the 'art of consideration for other riders and their horses'. Keen horses were allowed to work near the leader rather than being frustrated by being kept at the back of the group. This produced an underlying herd pecking order which the horses learned to accept.

Riders were never allowed to ride on ahead, being encouraged instead to ride with the safety and comfort of those on difficult horses in mind. Thoughtless riders who canter off without warning and leave others behind, regardless of the anxiety they leave in their wake, cause accidents and loss of nerve.

Teaching your horse to work with others so that you can both enjoy yourselves needs patience. Small and frequent introductions to other horses is one of the best ways of developing a calm mount. A regular companion for your horse is also a useful suggestion. After all, the horse who becomes over-excited on discovering itself to be suddenly part of a herd is only behaving like a natural horse would do on sighting its own kin.

Solo Riding

Some people like the support which riding with someone else can provide; others enjoy riding alone. Both activities should be part of the horse's experience, because each situation has its particular lessons. With the solo horse, you are more likely to experience problems such as its refusing to leave the stable or pass some frightening object *en route*, or its deciding that it is time to turn for home. Other horses may become bored with solitude, and lose their initiative.

The ideal horse will happily go on its own and still behave impeccably in company. To achieve this happy state, good schooling and logical discipline are the foundation stones, together with regular exposure to both situations. Riding in company can brighten the outlook of a lazy horse, while being ridden alone can calm the more excitable animal.

Jumping

The natural horse of the wild did not need jumping ability as part of its repertoire for survival. The ability of the modern horse to become airborne is an attribute it has acquired through its involvement with the human race, and is one that highlights its potential courage. The demands made on the present-day showjumper and event horse are considerable, as are the stresses of steeplechasing, where jumping in company adds other hazards. When we watch

these star performers we can see how much the horse has been changed through human intervention.

The idea of teaching a horse to jump may have originated when the enclosure system made artificial barriers across the country, thus making the journey from A to B more protracted. The horse that could take its rider over some of these obstacles would be able to make short cuts.

Some horses have an innate talent for this role, so it is perhaps not strictly true to say that the horse is not a natural jumper. What is unnatural is for it to carry a weight on its back, and to jump artificial-looking obstacles of all sizes and shapes. A horse soon learns to negotiate small hazards in a natural setting, such as fallen trees, a shallow ditch, or a bank. There are a few horses with particular intelligence and ability who take the law into their own hands once they have discovered the art of jumping out of their field. Once this habit is established it is virtually incurable, and poses a continual problem until the horse is stabled. Even then some horses can open box doors, and even those of their friends, so it is to be hoped that your field escapee does not also possess these delinquencies.

I would suggest that those riders who want to train their horse to jump should make mutual confidence and enjoyment their priorities. The horse's trust in the rider is vitally important, so the horse must learn that it will not be overstretched or frightened in any way. The novice horse can be introduced to the concept of jumping during country rides. Opportunities may present themselves in the form of tree trunks, low bushes, shallow ditches and banks. However, the size of the jump should be considered (do not attempt

An introduction to jumping without the rider's weight.

anything too big), as should the siting of the jump. Horses can also be wary of jumping from light foreground into a dark background; this can release the animal's primeval fears, and reminds us that the natural horse is never far away.

Coloured poles laid out on an arena or field is the next introductory step. This is a more artificial setting, but one in which the horse can learn to concentrate on where it is placing its feet. One pole only should be used to begin with, over which the horse should be asked to walk in both directions. Next place three poles, one behind the other, in parallel lines 1 yard (1 metre) apart. Do not use two poles, as the horse tends to jump them. At this stage the horse is learning to walk calmly over the poles. This gives it time to look at what it is doing, placing its feet neatly in the spaces in between the poles. When

this is achieved a rhythmical trot can be attempted; when this is established a small jump can be placed at the end of a row of four or perhaps six poles, about 3 yards (2.7 metres) beyond the last pole. This exercise produces a calm, confident approach to a fence. The exact measurements of trotting poles and fences used in introductory gymnastic work are available in other books.

A Rich Variety of Experience

As we have seen, outlets for the twentieth-century rider and horse have developed despite the declining acres of countryside available for riding. The evolution of one- and three-day eventing, and the opportunities available for cross-country riding,

145

Walking over one pole.

Walking over three poles.

Trotting over three poles.

Three poles with a jump.

Susan preparing a turn into a jump.

These scenes are very different from the riding of my youth, which left much to be desired in expertise. This was partly due to the scarcity of instruction, which meant that most of us learnt to control our mounts by trial and error. With luck one might become proficient enough to emerge in the hunting field, while agricultural shows and gymkhanas provided some variety. Now there is ample opportunity for enthusiasts to find a good instructor and to ride with much more elegance and tact, for which our horses must be grateful. There are still black spots in horse welfare, but those that seek to know more cast a ray of light on the horse's lot by setting a good example to others.

Whatever choice you make in your quest for pleasurable riding, do remember that the horse should share the enjoyment. It has limitations of intelligence, endurance and courage, and should not be

provide an alternative way of experiencing riding in the countryside. To complement the cross-country phase there is the discipline provided by the dressage test and showjumping. This combination requires a well-balanced, versatile horse with zest and courage.

Polo, hunter trials, team chases and hunting provide the thrills that fulfil some people. Various forms of racing, driving and long-distance riding also have their place in the horse-lover's calendar. However, it is not just the active participants who benefit now that modern technology can bring the lure of the horse into millions of homes. Its public appeal can be seen in the large crowds who faithfully gather at these events regardless of the weather.

Jumping a parallel.

Riding a dressage test in a downpour.

Indoor showjumping. (Photo: Sir John Forbes of Craigevar.)

Susan out for a gallop.

exploited. It must be kept fit enough to cope with the exercises required without becoming exhausted. You cannot pull a horse out of a field with its belly full of grass and expect it to be a star performer. Jumping enthusiasts in particular tend to get carried away and ask too much from their horses. This shows when their horses refuse to jump, and become excited and out of control. This sort of treatment could easily impair a horse's health and soundness. To know your horse's potential and limitations is one of the secrets of happy riding, whatever your preference happens to be.

My experience is that riders who enjoy learning reach their goals with less effort. If we keep reminding ourselves that the natural horse is still with us, we can learn to utilize its attributes and be tactful with those of them who demonstrate their survival instincts too readily. Knowing the horse and working sympathetically with it helps us to utilize its full potential. A confident, educated horse is a joy to take out and about at any time.

I recently asked one of my pupils what it was that her horse offered her. She replied that it gave her contentment, and that she could not imagine life without a horse. Learning to know the horse more deeply, she said, had made her realize that no two behaved alike. Learning that one horse could not be schooled to behave just like another had helped her to accept their individuality; this had helped to dissipate a sense of disappointment when training did not proceed as smoothly as she would have liked. My final question to her was, 'What do you think you offer the horse?' Her reply was, 'A happy and secure life, for as long as possible!'

150

11 Full Circle

The evolutionary patterns of horse and human have changed their roles enormously over the centuries, but certain basic factors remain unchanged. Human interference with the horse's life has always had a profound effect on its development, yet when seen at its best the contemporary horse is a remarkable animal.

In many ways the human race seems to have evolved too fast for its own good. While the mind races on, the body suffers as we lose touch with our need to stay in contact with the natural world. That subconscious urge to keep in contact with nature may be the main reason why the horse has become increasingly popular with an ever-wider range of people. The sport of kings is no longer exclusive to the privileged few, and many more people now have the opportunity to share the thrills and spills of racing, polo, show-jumping, eventing, driving competitions and hunting. The horse has emerged as a luxury rather than a necessity, and provides a form of therapy in the busy lives of twentieth-century humans.

It seems ironic that the horse, our main means of transport for so many centuries, now finds itself being transported long distances in a metal box before it can assume its original role as a means of transport. The sophisticated means of transport now available for the horse to get from A to B does not reduce the unnaturalness of the horse's experience: travelling in claustrophobic areas between partitions, combined with the constant movement, causes both exhaustion and trauma. To relieve the inevitable stress involved, every precaution should be taken to ensure that the horse has room for its head, neck and legs, so that it can adjust its balance. Protective poll and tail guards and leg bandages should be provided, and suitable rugs for the time of year. Water, food and rest should be given at regular intervals on long journeys.

As the horse's past usefulness as a means of transport on which civilization depended has declined in favour of the sporting or pleasure horse; its past contribution to our physical needs has been turned into a way of finding solace in a more stressful world. Few horses nowadays work all day long for their living, and most of them have become 'hobby horses', with whom to share our leisure time. As I see it, however, the horse is still the major contributor, and it seems appropriate to take stock of the relationship we have developed over the centuries. An overview of our present state of play can help us to foster more far-sighted and caring programmes for the species to whom we owe so much.

History may for centuries have been carried on the back of a horse, but it now proceeds on the wings of fast aeroplanes and cars, whose equivalent in horsepower is mind-blowing. And yet for all our so-called progress, it is obvious to me that the human race has still not discovered the wisdom of living in harmony. There is always some part of the world where wars are taking place, where violence is being meted out to fellow human beings; always there are those who are being oppressed by others. A recent example of our aggression came with the fighting in Croatia, which resulted in the Lippizaner stud being caught in the firing zone, causing the death and injury of many of the horses. After our long journey together through history, what have we done to acknowledge our debt to the horse, who has so often been the victim of our less-than-admirable natures?

There are some more hopeful signs, however. There is, for example, the inspiring work carried out by the Brooke Hospital for horses in Cairo. Mrs Geoffrey Brooke, the founder, set out to rescue the desperate ex-war horses she found in the city after the First World War, which claimed the lives of 260,000 mules and horses (mostly from malnutrition rather than from wounds as one might expect). Sadly, many survivors of these campaigns ended up in the Middle East where they faced appalling conditions, although some of them were lucky enough to be rescued by Mrs Brooke's caring concern. The hospital has continued its work, and has recently opened its doors in India. This good work goes on apace to recompense the horse for the human ignorance, poverty, cruelty and greed which have claimed the lives of so many fine animals.

Conserving the Feral Horse

The feral horse lives in the wild state but is descended from domestic horses that have escaped and then reverted to their natural life. The horses that were left behind by the Conquistadors provided the foundation stock of the herds now living on the plains of North America. These

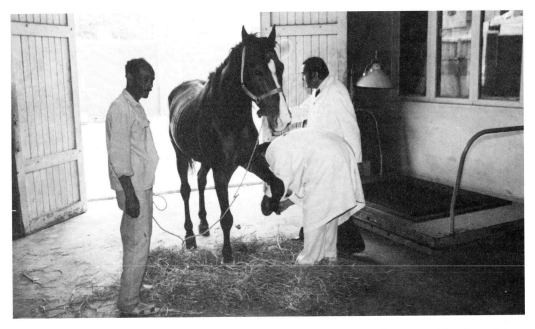

Veterinary treatment at the Brooke Hospital in Cairo. (Photos: The Brooke Hospital for Animals.)

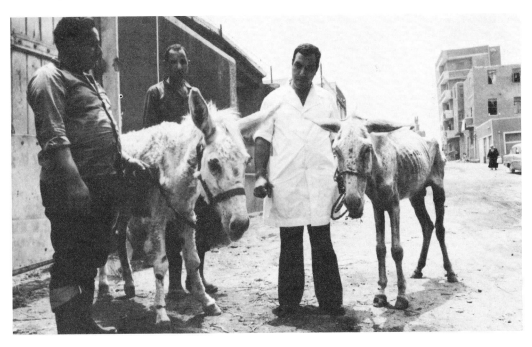

Patients waiting to be treated.

horses are referred to as mustangs. The brumbies of Australia are that continent's equivalent of the mustang, and like the mustangs their population is exceeding the support level of the land where they graze. Herds of these semi-wild horses are causing increasing difficulties for the farmers. They are culled by shooting them from helicopters or from the ground, during which many animals are wounded and left to die agonising deaths. The survivors are then rounded up and loaded into trailers, where long journeys to the abattoirs take a further toll on broken limbs, thirst, exhaustion and hunger.

Although mustangs and brumbies can become a problem, with careful management their numbers can be more humanely controlled. The United States Government has passed a law protecting these horses and providing a special region for them. Now, however, their numbers have exceeded the support level of that area and the horses are poaching on adjacent farmland for their food and water. In Wyoming, a Canadian vet operates a system for rounding up and corralling the horses before finding appropriate homes for them. The rounding up of wild horses is a very frightening process, and the foals look completely exhausted on their arrival at the corrals. The helicopters that help to drive them must increase the trauma for these animals, releasing all their instinctive fears about being hunted. The Canadian vet believes that the feral horse never becomes truly domesticated.

Nevertheless, this humane idea has prevented the shooting of these horses who, on arrival at their base, are prepared for adoption by having their feet pared and by being vaccinated. There is an air of dejection in the holding stations where these horses come to terms with their predicament. In one station the horses are cared for by prison inmates, a co-operation from which both prisoners and horses appear to benefit. One of the prisoners, when asked about his interaction with a particular horse, said that when the horse did not understand it became frightened, and then it got mad. To me, this demonstrates how, even in these strained circumstances, humans and horses can communicate successfully with each other. I find such integration heartening, and it goes some way to justifying the restriction of the wild horse for the sake of saving its life.

Capturing our Imagination

The horse has often been intimately involved with human ambitions, so it is hardly surprising that the modern horse often finds itself at the centre of media attention. Popular interest in horse sports has been fostered to the extent that world-class competition can be viewed at home by anyone with access to a television. Now we can all see the contemporary horse dancing like a ballerina in dressage events, jumping formidable obstacles on cross-country courses and completing clear rounds of show jumps like a superb athlete. We can see the team work of driven horses in competition and the endurance of long-distance riding. The dexterity of ponies has enthralled audiences who watch gymkhana games. One of the most moving contributions the horse has made to society is its co-operation with disabled riders. The horse is superb in this role, and has given these riders inspiration and hope as new doors have opened up before them in their relationship with the horse.

Selective breeding, intensive feeding and training programmes have produced some phenomenal equine performers, which have become stars in their own right. Perhaps part of their charisma is their special intelligence and their unique relationship with humans. Personality can never be defined and is a magical quality about which a judge friend of mine said, 'If your horse hasn't got it, don't bother showing it.'

We certainly all recognize the magnetism of horses like Red Rum and Desert Orchid. These horses, which have performed so gallantly, have captured everyone's imagination and have had their own fan clubs. It is sad to see them when they meet defeat, having revelled in so much limelight. These evolved horses give much pleasure and obviously enjoy doing so, and are one of the brighter aspects of our relationship with horses.

But every sport has its drop-outs, and even treasured ponies and horses outgrow their usefulness. Equine old age pensioners pose a growing problem, especially now there is a dearth of knackers and difficulty in disposing of their remains. Responsibility for old horses is enormous, and can tax the owners financially. In some cases these horses are lucky enough to end their lives in dignity but, alas, too many end up as discarded wrecks. Horse owners need to think very carefully before taking on such a commitment, for the least we can do is to release our equine friends peacefully when the time comes.

There are various sanctuaries for old and neglected horses which do marvellous rescue work. These charities carry an enormous financial burden in supporting these animals for life, and those horses and donkeys that are fortunate enough to find a home with them are indeed blessed.

Finding freedom on horseback. (Photo: Angela Stocks, Riding for the Disabled Association, Glenfarg Group.)

It is sad to think that ignorance and greed make such places necessary in this day and age.

Return to Nature

I should like to move towards a conclusion of this evolutionary story of horse and human by returning to good news, held in a letter from J.M. Knowles, the director of Marwell Zoological Park in Hampshire. Mr Knowles sent me a contribution authored by himself and his staff biologist for a publication on wild equids which is being produced by the Wild Equid

155

Specialist Group of the World Conservation Union. He writes:

As far as the reintroduction of the wild horse to Mongolia is concerned, I have every hope that this will go forward in the relatively near future. This is a truly international effort, and my visit to Mongolia is being followed up as I write, by the Curator of the Cologne 200, who is the co-ordinator of the European Breeding Programme for this species, and Professor Stubbe of the University of Halle, who is an expert on the ecology of Mongolia. One of the exciting aspects of this programme which, unlike other reintroduction programmes that I have looked at for other species, makes this one possible and indeed certain, is the enthusiasm of the Mongolians themselves.

It is still our hope that the first horses may go to Mongolia during the course of this year, and from this start will develop what will probably be a ten-year programme involving the establishment of a number of herds in a 10,000 hectare enclosure, at the end of which time one or more herds will be released into the complete wild. One of our problems of course is the fact that the horses will hybridize with domestic horses, and hence the need for fencing and eventually the removal of all domestic horses, other than geldings, from the Gobi Park B.

Further research is planned with a view to transferring the first animals to Mongolia in the early summer of 1993.

The global effort to redress the demise of one of the horse's ancestors is indeed encouraging, and shows a developing awareness of the need to preserve the heritage of the wild. Such projects show that caring custody of the rich heritage we have squandered is possible. In this setting the horse appears to have come full circle, and so perhaps have we.

To sum up my feelings about this, I should like to quote an extract from a poem by Evelyn Nolt, published in Sir George Trevelyan's book *Magic Casements*:

Man, tread softly on the Earth
What looks like dust
Is also stuff of which galaxies are made.
The green of Earth's great trees and
    simple grasses
Is the same music played in red
Throughout our trunks and limbs
The first eye broadcast thought.
Function is the eye of dust
Fragrance is the flower's eye
The furred and feathered eye is freedom
If we cannot see that dust looks back at us
If we will not see thought in the animal
It is because we bind our eyes
To stay Evolution's seeing.
O blessed Earth.
O patient Earth
We struggle upward to the Sun
Forgetting what we as dust knew
Forgetting what we as flower saw
Forgetting what we as animal are
Forgetting humanness is synthesis
Of dust, flower, animal and something
more.
O Earth, living, breathing, thinking Earth
On the day we treasure you
As you have treasured us
Humanness is born.

Does the past have any meaning for you? Is there anything to be learnt from our own and the horse's evolution? And what does the horse symbolize in our modern society, now it is no longer a utilitarian necessity?

Recently my brother and I were discussing our experiences with horses we had owned, and I found myself asking him why he rode at all. He replied, 'Freedom.' His was an interesting answer when we consider the horse's loss of liberty in the service it gives human beings. I wonder how you would answer this question.

A twentieth-century descendant of Equus caballus.

Many more people now have a chance to enjoy the horse's companionship and mobility. Where once there were few civilian instructors, now there are teachers everywhere to cater for all levels of competence. When I first came to Scotland I was the only freelance coach on the circuit; now good instruction is available to all those who seek it. It pays to be selective for your own sake and that of the horse; the relationship between you and your teacher is very important, as is the condition of the horse that you ride. I believe that when you are ready, the right teacher will appear.

There is no end to the learning process for those with open minds. Learning to be a more perceptive and co-ordinated partner with the horse is not an end in itself.

With your own progress you also help the horse's emancipation, and harmony between you both can have a far-reaching influence on the world around you.

In this book, I have endeavoured to describe the natural horse and the background tapestry of its evolution, through which is interwoven its relationship with humans. Together they have moved through history and on to the twentieth-century stage, from which they can review the injustices and benefits that the horse has experienced in human hands, as well as the harmony that mutual trust can bring to this unique relationship. What the story means to you personally will depend on how you interpret the horse's evolution, its presence in your life, and its role in the future.

Further Reading

Bongianni, Mario *The Macdonald Encyclopedia of Horses* Macdonald and
    Co. Publishers Ltd (1988)
Cooper, Jilly *Animals in War* William Heinemann Ltd (1983)
Edward, Betty *Drawing with the Right Side of Your Brain* William Collins &
    Co. Ltd (1979)
Edwards, Hartley *The Saddle* J.A. Allen & Co. Ltd (1990)
Hedlund, Gunnar *This is Riding* George G. Harrap & Co. Ltd (1981)
McBane, Susan (Ed.) *The Horse and the Bit* The Crowood Press (1988)
Rees, Lucy *The Horse's Mind* Stanley Paul (1984)
Rose, Mary *The Horsemaster's Notebook* Peter Barker Publishing Ltd (1972)
Savoie, Jane *That Winning Feeling* J.A. Allen & Co. Ltd (1992)
Shone, Ronald *Creative Visualisation* Thorsons Publishers Ltd (1984)
Spooner, Glenda (Ed.) *For the Love of Horses: The Diaries of Mrs Geoffrey Brooke*
    Brooke Hospital for Animals, London (1962)
Stanier, Sylvia *The Art of Lungeing* J.A. Allen & Co. Ltd (1986)
The Pony Club Manual of Horsemanship Threshold Books Ltd (1950)
Townley, Audrey *Natural Riding* The Crowood Press (1990)
Trevelyan, George *Magic Casements* Coventure Ltd (1980)
Tuke, Diana R. *Bit by Bit* J.A. Allen & Co. Ltd (1965)

Index

Page numbers in italics refer to illustrations